Educating Citizens:

A Democratic Socialist Agenda for Canadian Education

Educating Citizens:

OUR SCHOOLS

Education Publishing

OUR SELVES

A Democratic Socialist Agenda
for Canadian Education

Ken Osborne

Photos by Ursula Heller

Canadian Cataloguing in Publication Data

Osborne, Kenneth, 1936-
Educating Citizens

(Our Schools/Our Selves Monograph Series No.1)
Bibliography: p.
ISBN 0-921908-00-8

1. Education - Canada - Aims and Objectives.
2. Education - Canada - Curricula.
3. Socialism and education - Canada.
I. Our Schools/Our Selves Education Foundation. II. Title. III. Series

LA412.7.073 1988   370.11'5'0971   C89-093038-4

This book is published by Our Schools/Our Selves Education
Foundation, 1698 Gerrard Street East, Toronto, Ontario, M4L 2B2. For
subscribers to **Our Schools/Our Selves: a magazine for Canadian
education activists** it is issue #2. The content of future issues can be
found at the back of the book, along with subscription forms.

The subscription series **Our Schools/Our Selves** (ISSN 0840-7339) is
published 8 times a year. Second class mail Registration No. 8010.
Design: Ritchie Donaghue & Associates.
Typesetting: David Clandfield.
Printed in Canada by Del Charters Litho, Brampton, Ontario.

Educating Citizens is published with the financial assistance of the
Douglas-Coldwell Foundation.

TABLE OF CONTENTS

CHAPTER 1 : EDUCATING CITIZENS
1. Citizenship and the Schools 1
2. Citizenship and Participation 2
3. Citizenship and Socialism 5
4. Citizenship and Capitalism... 7
5. Citizenship and Nationalism 10
6. Nation, Class and Education 12

CHAPTER 2 : RETHINKING EDUCATIONAL GOALS
1. The Needs of Society and the Needs of the Individual 15
2. Educational Goals in Canada 17
3. A Democratic Socialist Curriculum 23
4. Community Involvement and Service 27

CHAPTER 3 : A WORKING-CLASS CURRICULUM
1. Class and Learning 33
2. Working-Class Students and the Academic Curriculum 35
3. Working-Class Curriculum 38
4. The Community-Based Curriculum 40
5. A Divided Curriculum 42
6. The Common Curriculum 44
7. A Democratic Socialist Approach 46
8. The Question of Pedagogy 49

CHAPTER 4 : NATION, CITIZENSHIP AND CURRICULUM
1. Democratic Socialism and National Education 53
2. What Should Students Know About Canada?..................... 58
3. Canadian Studies and World Studies 66
4. Active Citizenship and Democratic Socialist Education 72

BIBLIOGRAPHY 76

Think about the kind of world you want to live and work in. What do you need to build that world? Demand that your teachers teach you that.

Peter Kropotkin

... it is a serious matter what sort of men the schoolmasters are to be, especially those of the elementary schools. They will be able to do more in a day for any creed or principle they hold than the House of Commons could do in a whole parliament... The Socialist leaders already perceive what a splendid field the elementary schools afford for their peculiar propaganda. What better career can they offer to their sons and daughters than to enter the teaching profession and in a discreet way play the socialist missionary?

W.R. Lawson, *John Bull and his Schools* (1908)

I have always felt an urgency, sometimes a thwarted urgency in Canadian life—the urgency of unfinished business. I have always felt that whereas the Fourth of July celebrated something that has already happened, July First celebrates something still happening.

M. Ross, *The Impossible Sum of Our Traditions* (1986)

PREFACE

This book began as a response to an invitation to weave together the themes of class, nation and education in a Canadian setting. After various shifts of emphasis it has ended as a discussion of the contribution of education to citizenship and democratic socialism in Canada.

The Canadian left has over the years paid remarkably little attention to the actual content of education. Indeed, it is fair to say that neither the C.C.F., the N.D.P., nor any other group on the left has ever had a coherent education policy. Apart from occasional bursts of concern about militarism, sexism, racism, or anti-labour bias, the school curriculum has gone largely unquestioned.

The N.D.P., in particular, has concentrated on achieving greater equality of access and opportunity so that women, native people, and working class people generally can get their share of the benefits that are presumed to flow from education. In doing so, however, the N.D.P. has implicitly treated the content of education as unproblematic. Education, it seems, is a good thing: the priority is to get more of it.

This lack of attention to curriculum questions is especially surprising since socialism both demands and depends upon a transformation of values. Such socialist values as cooperation, participation, personal autonomy, and a sense of community do not appear out of thin air. They have to be acquired. Conservatives and liberals have long realized this and have shaped the schools accordingly, so that the capitalist ethic of competitive individualism is now strongly entrenched and is learned early in life. If the old vision of the cooperative commonwealth, which retains its relevance today, is to become a reality, then education will have an important role to play. This book is an attempt to outline what this role might be.

Its argument derives heavily from personal experience and from contemporary educational debates. Although the Canadian left has paid little attention to curriculum questions, educational theorists and researchers have devoted a good deal of energy to them. Recent years, for example, have seen a rebirth of Marxist and other socialist analyses of education, although they have not had the impact one might have expected. Academic territorialism has meant that often these analyses have been confined to university departments of education— and they are not common even there. They have often been written in ponderous and complicated language which has restricted their reader-ship. They have been much stronger on analysis and criticism than on suggestions for action. Nonetheless, this book draws heavily upon them and anyone who wishes to pursue these arguments—presented here very briefly and simply—will find them worth reading in more detail.

This book is intended, however, to be not another contribution to educational philosophy but a spur to educational practice. Or rather it attempts to combine philosophy and practice so that one contributes to the other. It has been written for all those, on the left and elsewhere, who are interested in education but are not necessarily familiar with the main themes of recent education debate.

I am responsible for the arguments the book contains, including any weaknesses it might have. Whatever strengths it possesses are due in large part to George Martell whose advice, criticism and support were always constructive and helpful and much needed. Thanks also to David Clandfield for invaluable editorial advice and assistance. Finally, my thanks to the Douglas-Coldwell foundation for their generous support of this book.

Chapter 1

Educating Citizens

Citizenship and the Schools

Education and citizenship have long been connected in Canada. From their very beginnings schools were intended to Canadianize the young. By the early 1900's education had lost much of its earlier association with academic learning and high culture and was linked instead with training and social efficiency. The Winnipeg School Board nicely described this new approach in 1913:

> Until a comparatively recent period the schools were organized on purely academic lines and the avowed aim of education was culture and discipline. This aim has, however, been greatly enlarged within the past few years, by including within its scope the development of a sense of social and civic duty, the stimulation of national and patriotic spirit, the promotion of public health, and direct preparations for the occupations of life.

Little effort is required for us to read in these words a concern less for the welfare of individual students than for the survival and maintenance of existing forms of society. Children were expected to learn their social and civic duty, to acquire a patriotic spirit, to be prepared for the occupations of life: to learn their place in life and to keep their place.

Traditionally, Canadian educators have seen citizenship in passive terms such as these. The emphasis has been upon loyalty, obedience and conformity for most students, with a select few being encouraged to think for themselves, to act independently, to take control of their own lives—all, of course, within the larger purposes of the social order. Such a distinction serves the broader social distinction in capitalism between the few who make the decisions and give the orders and the many who accept and follow them.

This state of affairs is reflected in many everyday features of school practice. For example, one report card, used in the assessment of elementary school students' general behaviour, requires teachers to adjudge the degree of truth in the following statements about each student's behaviour:
- gets along with others;
- uses time to good advantage;
- completes assignments;
- works quietly and independently;
- listens well;
- is dependable;
- produces neat work;
- takes criticism and disappointment well.

It is difficult to imagine a set of qualities that better describes the diligent, dutiful worker, especially when nothing at all is said about such things as creativity, originality or critical insight. It would, after all, be simple enough to design a report card containing these latter categories. Cooperative and disciplined work habits are fine qualities, but they need to be linked to active and critical participation within the larger society if students are to keep their dignity.

A similar emphasis upon passive obedience can be found in schools' disciplinary practices, which, almost without exception, emphasize doing what one is told and not rocking the boat. Similar messages are often embedded in teaching methods, which do not encourage students to think for themselves, to use their imagination, or to exercise independence, but rather to follow instructions, to fill in the blanks, to copy down what they are told. Educational research confirms this, showing that the majority of students spend their time following (or sometimes resisting) teachers' instructions, and only rarely in exercising their own judgment or working independently.

In this framework, citizenship is seen as playing one's assigned part in the existing scheme of things, no questions asked.

Citizenship and Participation

In the world outside the school, citizenship is a changing, dynamic concept. It is not something automatically conferred as a reward for good behaviour. It is defined in the process of seeking to attain and exercise it. Historically, citizenship is the result of struggle.

The right to vote; the right to organize; the right to equality before the law; in fact, all the rights we now enjoy had to be won; they were not conferred without struggle or conflict. Ample testimony for this can be found in the history of both the labour movement and the women's movement. Moreover, citizenship rights cannot always be taken for granted. The history of their achievement is not one of uninterrupted progress but of moments of expansion and retrenchment. Even now, such rights as the right to organize and the right to strike cannot be taken for granted.

Citizenship, then, must be defined in active not passive terms. It demands participation and involvement at all levels of society. In reality, however, such citizenship is confined to a minority. The higher people are on the socio-economic ladder, the more politically involved and effective they are likely to be. One investigator into political participation in Canada has described his findings in this way:

> Although lawyers, doctors, businessmen and other professionals constitute fewer than ten per cent of the Canadian workforce, they occupy almost three-quarters of the seats in the House of Commons and two-thirds of the offices in local party organizations. Blue-collar workers, in contrast, comprise nearly half of the population but hold fewer than ten per cent of the positions either in local parties or in parliament. (Mishler, 1979, p.95)

There are obviously many reasons for this mockery of democracy—a mockery that appears all the more blatant when one takes into account the under-representation of women, native people and minorities in Canada's political and economic institutions—but the schools' inability to put their educational ideals into practice has at least something to do with it.

It is high time for us to take the concept of active citizenship seriously and to insist that it apply to everyone. For democratic socialists, above all, the goal is to establish a society that goes beyond the representative principle to embrace and encourage the principles of participation at all levels. And such principles are important for both individual and social reasons.

At the *individual* level, participation offers a means of repairing the break that has separated the individual from the community and of reducing the sense of powerlessness and alienation that characterizes

3

so much of contemporary life. In C.B. Macpherson's words, what is needed is "a change in people's consciousness (or unconsciousness), from seeing themselves and acting as essentially consumers to seeing themselves and acting as exerters and enjoyers of the exertion and development of their capacities." At the *social* level, participation will work to restore a sense of community for, in participating, people will work with others. Naturally, this can lead to conflict as easily as to consensus, but there is no reason why conflict should be socially destructive.

The social value of participation was well described by John Stuart Mill, who pointed out that when a citizen engaged in public affairs, he or she had to "weigh interests not his own; to be guided, in the case of conflicting claims, by another rule than his private partialities; to apply at every turn principles and maxims which have for their reason of existence the common good."(Thompson, 1976, pp.36-43) At the same time, a society that accepts and encourages participation is probably a society that will strive to reduce social and economic inequalities. In Macpherson's words again, "low participation and social inequality are so bound up with each other that a more equitable and humane society requires a more participatory political system."(Macpherson, 1976, p.99)

There are obvious implications in all this for education. In the first place, the schools must make it possible for students to gain the knowledge, skills and dispositions that will make it possible for them to exercise their rights of participation and to acquire them when they are withheld or denied. This means treating citizenship not as something static but as a contested, dynamic and ever-changing right which must be struggled for and exercised if it is to be realized.

This will be accomplished, in part, by teaching students about past and present struggles for rights in Canada and elsewhere; how they have been and are being both protected and denied; and how rights have been and can be defined in different societies. Three examples that no curriculum should ignore are those of the labour movement, the women's movement and the struggle against racism.

As always, knowledge alone is not enough. It is perfectly possible to know a great deal about the history and current state of the struggle for full citizenship without ever lifting a finger to do anything about it, whether for oneself or for others. Participation, therefore, is not simply another topic in the curriculum, no matter how important. It must also be embodied in the way schools and classrooms are organized, in the way that teachers teach and students learn.

In more general terms, the curriculum must be organized to show students the world as it is, not a sanitized or ideologically bound view of it; to show them also how it might be, by giving them a sense of alternatives; and to give them the skills that will help to change it.

Citizenship and Socialism

For democratic socialists participation is not something to be pursued simply for its own sake. It is a fundamental component of any worthwhile conception of citizenship, but it must be combined with a social vision. The struggle for democratic socialism is inspired by a vision of the future. This does not mean that it has a grand design or precise blueprint according to which it intends to squeeze people into a predetermined mould. Grand designs have a way of becoming straitjackets into which people are forced against their will by those who have the "correct" ideological insights. This is not the way that democratic socialists see the future, for in their eyes democracy is as important as socialism. Democracy without socialism is only half-formed; and socialism without democracy is unthinkable. Democratic socialism has no blueprints, no secret plans. It does, however, have a vision of the good society as a cooperative commonwealth, in which all citizens work equally together for the common good, and this vision shapes the socialist view of the present, informing both its criticism of existing society and its sense of the action needed to get from the present to the future.

In looking to the future while not ignoring the present, democratic socialism has much in common with education, for it too is a future-oriented activity. There is a long and continuing debate in educational circles between those who see it as primarily preparing children for the future and those who see it as dealing with children as they exist here and now. In fact, educational practice inevitably consists of both and, to a large extent, the debate on both sides has missed the point. The whole educational enterprise concerns both present and future. Teachers cannot avoid wondering what the future holds for their students and whether the substance and style of their teaching will affect that future.

But all this presupposes another question: what kind of future do we want for our students? It is in this shared concern for the future that education and democratic socialism find common ground. The concern has become especially important since Hiroshima and Nagasaki, as we have come to realize that we hold the power to destroy future life forever. Students realize this at an early age. Researchers have found in country after country, including Canada, that the prospect of nuclear war is among the two or three greatest fears that children have and that this fear begins at a remarkably early age. We now commonly find that teenagers have a bleak view of the future and, in many cases, are even wondering whether there will be a future. For many, this pessimism breeds feelings of powerlessness, alienation, apathy and cynicism.

One can easily understand and sympathize with these feelings when one looks at the world as it presents itself to children and young people, or rather as it is presented through television, magazines and newspapers. It is no surprise if they look at the world they are inheriting and are depressed by what they see.

Thus, the answer to the question—what kind of world do we want for our students?—must be that, in the most basic sense, we want them to have a world to inhabit. This means teaching them whatever is needed in the way of knowledge, skills and values to ensure that the world is not destroyed before they inherit it, whether by nuclear war or environmental catastrophe. As things stand, we seem to be faced with a choice between destroying the world in thirty minutes or a couple of centuries—and students are fully aware of this. We must then do all that we can in education to open other options and, at the same time, to ensure that the survival and prosperity of one part of the world do not depend upon the poverty and exploitation of another. Students should learn, for example, that their enjoyment of a hamburger might require clearing the South American rainforest to make way for beef pasture, with disastrous consequences both for the local population and the ecology of the planet. They must realize that, thanks in large part to capitalism, the world has become an interlocking system, so that its survival will depend not only on avoiding nuclear war and treating the environment with respect, but also on treating all parts of it and all its people fairly.

Democratic socialists want a future that allows students to live full and rewarding lives. They should be able to find jobs that are meaningful, that are both socially useful and personally fulfilling, and that do not create a hierarchy of unequal status and reward. They should

6

be able to enjoy and contribute to a sense of community, to work with others for the mutual benefit of all, not finding themselves condemned to a life in which their enjoyments and benefits can be obtained only at others' expense. They should be entitled to equality of rights and treatment, in everyday life as well as in theory. They should be able to live without fear of violence, insecurity, unemployment or any of the shadows that cloud the future. They should be in control of their own lives, neither dominating others, nor being dominated. They should have the skills and the commitment to participate in public affairs so that when decisions are made, they are made democratically and fairly. To put it simply, they should be able, as William Morris once said, to make the most of their talents in all directions.

For all this to occur, society will have to be organized according to different principles. Inequality will have to give way to equality; competitiveness to cooperation; individual gain and self-interest to a sense of community and the common good; profit to social use; private ownership of the means of production to democratic control; exploitation to stewardship; aggression to peace.

This kind of socialism has much in common with and much to learn from feminism and environmentalism. It is not a socialism that seeks its roots in state-power and central planning but in human emancipation at all levels and in all dimensions. No one knows just how to get there. There are no magic plans or secret formulas. It is a matter of working through present problems with an eye to the future. And in this process, education has an important, if limited role to play.

If education is to achieve this, however, the schools must come to terms with their history, for they were originally created to prepare students not for many-sided and rewarding lives, but for specific slots in a divided and unequal society. Schools were intended not so much to educate as to train. Their task was not to open minds but to mould them to fit a particular pattern. To their credit, many teachers rejected and continue to reject this task, but to do so means constantly challenging the history that shapes their work.

Citizenship and Capitalism

Ever since the Industrial Revolution, schools in capitalist societies have been assigned a particular role: the maintenance and re-production of capitalism and the values on which it depends. As indus-

7

trialization proceeded, more and more industrialists came to understand the importance of producing the kind of personality that would freely integrate itself into the new society, and, in this task of shaping popular consciousness, the schools were central.

One of the more serious problems facing the early industrialists was labour discipline. It was no easy task to transform men and women accustomed to an agrarian rhythm into people who would govern themselves by clock and bell. Agrarian rhythms were largely tied to the cycle of physical nature: getting up at dawn, going to bed at dusk, working hard at particular times such as seeding and harvest, taking it more easily at others. There was an attitude to time that had little to do with the clock. Landes writes of the peasant who "in moments of affluence ... lived for the day; gave no thought to the morrow; spent much of his meagre pittance in the local inn or alehouse; caroused the Saturday of pay, the Sabbath Sunday and 'Holy Monday' as well; dragged himself reluctantly back to work Tuesday, warmed to the task Wednesday, and laboured furiously Thursday and Friday to finish in time for another long weekend."(Landes, 1969, p.2)

Such workers were obviously not promising material for the new factories, which demanded that they be conscious of clock time, that they work at the pace of machines, and that they govern themselves by prescribed routines. Their rejection of this order was a serious problem for nineteenth-century employers, who explored various solutions to it: coercion and harsh discipline; paternalism; the use of women and children who might be more docile; the use of technology to de-skill and simplify work to make workers easily replaceable; and, not least, the use of education as a form of training, an approach with a long tradition. The Abbé Galiéni, in attacking Rousseau's child-centred views, wrote in the 1760's that

> Education is the same for man and beast. It can be reduced to two principles, to learn to put up with injustice, to learn to endure ennui. What does one do when one breaks in a horse? Left to himself, the horse ambles, trots, gallops, walks but does it when he wishes, as he pleases. We teach him to move thus and thus, contrary to his desires, against his own desires, against his own instinct—there is the injustice: we make him keep at it for a couple of hours—there is the ennui. It is just the same thing when we make a child

learn Latin or Greek or French. The intrinsic utility of it is not the main point. The aim is that he should habituate himself to another person's will ... it is a question of learning the weariness of concentrating one's attention on the matter in hand.(Boyd, 1912, pp.306-7)

Thus arose the structure of punctuality, diligence, obedience and politeness that came to characterize the schools. Thus arose the textbooks' emphasis on the importance of being "hard-working, temperate, and peaceable." Thus arose also a curriculum and a pedagogy designed to make sure that students' ideas were appropriate to their station. As the historians of education have shown us, the advocates and promoters of compulsory schooling had many motives, but among them was a concern for control and the preservation of the emerging capitalist order.

Until fairly recently, capitalist education was deliberately kept at an elementary level for most students. Those in power thought that it was unnecessary, even dangerous, for working people to be taught more than the barest rudiments of the three R's, together with a certain quantity of approved general knowledge. In the nineteenth century, there was considerable debate in some European countries over whether the working class would abuse its new-found literacy by reading dangerous and seditious literature. From time to time working-class adults took matters into their own hands and created mechanics' institutes and similar institutions to teach the knowledge that they wanted, rather than the knowledge that their betters thought appropriate for them. The curriculum was something of an ideological battleground, as the capitalists and their allies sought to use it to channel and control working-class aspirations and attitudes, while working people tried to take control of it for themselves.

By the middle of the twentieth century, the principle of "secondary education for all," and not just for those who were thought to be bright, had been established in most countries, largely through the efforts of trade unions, and socialist and social-democratic parties. However, the acceptance of this principle did little or nothing to alter a system that had designed different curricula for different kinds of students. The policy of secondary education for all was perfectly compatible with the apparently common-sense notion that different students had different abilities, aptitudes or interests, with some being

9

primarily academic, others technical or commercial, and yet others vocational or, for want of a better word, "general." The schools grew into a system for sorting students into different slots, allegedly in their own best interests but in reality to serve the purposes of the economic system, while at the same time making the process seem natural, inevitable and even scientific, thanks to the use of intelligence and aptitude tests, guidance counsellors and other alleged experts.

Citizenship and Nationalism

The nineteenth century saw the emergence of nationalism as an important political force. It led to the dissolution of centuries-old empires and to the creation of such new states as Italy, Germany and the countries of Latin America. Nationalism assigned an important role to schools. National citizens had to be created and nationalist ideas had to be cultivated and, in both cases, the schools would do the job. As David Goggin, Superintendent for Education of the Northwest Territories, put it in 1891: "While the church was in the ascendant, education was modelled in accordance with religious needs. Now that the state is in the ascendant we may expect education to be moulded more in accordance with political—I use the word in the best sense—needs."(Chaiton & McDonald, 1977, p.67) And these political needs had largely to do with creating and maintaining national unity, national awareness and a whole collection of what were deemed to be appropriate national values.

This description applies to Canada only in part. Popular nationalism had little to do with the creation of Confederation in 1867, which was a political agreement worked out by political elites. It did not supersede or eradicate regional and local loyalties, but rather accepted them and struggled to accommodate them. Thus, education has remained a provincial responsibility and Canada is one of the very few countries without a ministry of education or any sort of formal educational presence at the federal level. From the beginning, however, there have been those who are opposed to this state of affairs and who would prefer a national, not a provincial, educational policy. As Goggin put it in 1904: "Education within the provinces tends to become parochial in spirit and narrow in view, while the type of education, which it is the function of the school of the school to build up, should have a national rather than a provincial outlook."(Chaiton & McDonald, 1977, p.68)

10

This national outlook was to go beyond an unemotional analysis of the national scene, it was to be a celebration of greatness, whether real or potential. This attitude can be clearly seen in the words of George Ross, Ontario's Minister of Education, in 1892:

> I have perused with great care the various histories in use in all the provinces of the Dominion, and I have found them merely to be provincial histories, without reference to our common country... Can't we agree upon certain broad features common to the whole of this Dominion with which we can indoctrinate our pupils, so that when a child takes up the history of Canada, he feels that he is not simply taking up the history of Canada, such as the old Canada was, but that he is taking up the history of a great country? "(Chaiton & McDonald, 1977, pp. 14-15)

This vision of Canada as "a great country" was held by many of those who hoped that Confederation would lead to a new nationality: "If we desire to build up a strong nation, having a national sentiment that will be purely Canadian, the work must be done in our public schools.""(Chaiton & McDonald, 1977, pp. 73-4)

One plank in the nationalist education platform, then, was the call for a vision of Canada that saw the country as more than the sum of its parts, that went beyond local, provincial or regional interests, and that thought in terms of a Canadian nationality. In the words of Manitoba's Minister of Education in 1920: "A teacher should be a teacher, not for one province only but for all Canada. Our schools should not be Manitoba schools, but Canadian schools located in Manitoba."(Tomkins, 1986, p.147) The same argument has been heard in recent years. In 1968, the Royal Commission on Bilingualism and Biculturalism complained that "Canadian history is taught not from the national viewpoint but from the provincial," and pointed particularly to the "two different worlds" of Anglophone and Francophone Canadians. In Quebec, the Parent Commission commented, "If history is a science aiming at an objective interpretation, it is difficult to understand why it is taught from two extremely different perspectives... both groups have everything to gain from a good knowledge of the whole history of Canada, and the main lines of the programme could be the same for all."(Milburn, 1972, p.116) In 1968, Hodgetts condemned the schools for "overemphasizing provincial concerns and inadvertently neglecting legitimate national interests."(Hodgetts, 1968, p.15)

From their beginning, then, Canadian schools have seen citizenship in national—and even nationalist—terms. Part of their task has been to produce Canadians. For democratic socialists this Canadian dimension of citizenship is crucial. Students deserve to live in the world as Canadians, not to become Americans by default and to see the country slip away from beneath their feet. This is important not because Canada is imbued with some cosmic significance nor because it embodies some mystic notion of race and heritage. Such ideas, it is to be hoped, died in the Second World War. The argument here is much more down-to-earth: Canada represents a distinct society; whatever its faults, it has the potential to become a genuinely open, just and democratic community; the alternative to its continued existence is not some utopia of international solidarity, but absorption into the United States, or at least its complete conversion to American values. In such a context, we can paradoxically do more, even for the cause of internationalism, by working hard to ensure the independent existence of Canada. Unfortunately, Canada's existence can never quite be taken for granted, and the nature of Canadian society, both as it is and as it should be, is subject to a variety of competing interpretations. Schools have a central role to play in familiarizing students with the contours and significance of this continuing debate.

Nation, Class and Education

In Canada, where national awareness cannot always be taken for granted, education has a vital task to perform. Denis Smith has noted that "nationalism in Canada ... remains the precarious nationalism of a diverse community that is still only dimly aware of itself, existing always in the American shadow and beset by doubt."(Smith, 1985, p.1200) In these circumstances, Canadian schools have a duty to make students aware of the implications of citizenship in Canadian society, as it is and as it might be. Not least, they have a role to play in redefining the whole concept of citizenship, and its implications for education. Since national awareness and identity are not so much givens, but rather subjects of continuing debate, this means not inducting students into some official orthodoxy but rather initiating them into what might be called the great debate of who we are, where we are and where we should be going.

This concern for national citizenship has its problems, not least of which is its tendency to obscure and ignore division and conflict. Canadian history textbooks, for example, have often omitted important aspects of their subject in their concern to portray the process of "building the Canadian nation." Part of the impulse behind the push to include Canadian Studies in curricula in the 1970's derived from a fear that Canada was in danger of falling apart. The three main problems that Hodgetts and others in the Canadian Studies movement identified were English/French relations, U.S. economic and cultural penetration, and regionalism--all of which were said to be made more dangerous by widespread public ignorance and apathy, especially among the young.

These problems were and are clearly important, but in formulating them Hodgetts ignored the existence of another kind of division altogether, that deriving from inequalities in wealth, status and power— in short, from social class. There is not space here to discuss the intricacies of the concept of class, nor to describe the inequalities of wealth and power in Canada; they have been documented many times. We now know that, in Canada as in other countries, education is an integral part of these inequalities. Middle class students, for example, get far more benefit from education than do their working-class counterparts. More fundamentally, schools and their curricula often serve to perpetuate and legitimize inequalities of social class, either by refusing to deal with them or by making them appear to be natural and inevitable.

We are increasingly aware that curricula have either ignored, stereotyped or otherwise portrayed women, native people and ethnic minorities in ways that demonstrate cultural bias and that they have reinforced the mutual misconceptions of Anglophone and Francophone Canadians. What is rarely discussed is how school curricula deal, or fail to deal, with social class in Canada.

Studies in Canada and elsewhere have repeatedly shown that many working-class students do less well in school than they should or could. Ironically, those who do succeed in school only reinforce the impression that schools are indeed genuinely open institutions in which those who do less well have only themselves (or their parents) to blame. This obscures the schools' underlying class bias that serves to keep most working-class children in their place while recruiting a few to a higher social rank.

13

In any event, there is no doubt that school curricula do scant justice to the culture and experience of working-class children and that they portray Canada as classless. Such a view must be discarded if curricula are to play their part in educating children for the active, participating, critical citizenship that a democratic socialist Canada needs, a task that also requires schools to discard the largely conservative mission they have assumed over the years.

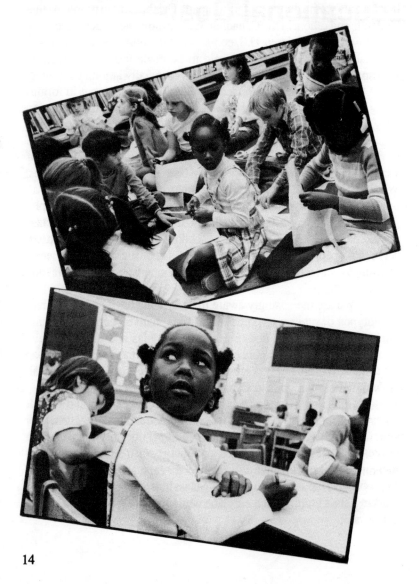

Chapter 2

Rethinking Educational Goals

The Needs of Society and the Needs of the Individual

Schools are expected to serve two purposes: first, they have to meet the needs of society and, second, they have to meet the needs of individual students. In capitalist societies, these needs are often in conflict, especially in the case of working class students: for to the extent that schools feel the pressure to sort students into different programmes, to identify their alleged aptitudes and intelligence, to decide who is "academic material" and who is not, they neglect the ideal of giving all students, without exception, an all-round education that will enable them to make full use of all their talents and even to discover talents that no-one knew they had. In capitalist societies, schools are forced to put the needs of a stratified society a long way ahead of the individual. The process is not always smooth or uncontested and the schools often resist conversion into job-training centres; however, their own commitment to provide every student with an appropriate education, as defined by the specialists in testing and guidance, leads them to place students in programmes that are self-fulfilling prophecies and that largely serve the priorities of the economic system. Such programmes do not educate, but train and socialize. Their goal is not the truly educational one of freeing students from preconceived ideas and conventional wisdom, of widening their horizons and showing them the world as it is and as it might be, but rather of fitting them into what exists, of taking the status quo for granted and seeking to adapt students to it. The educational goal of helping students to think critically about the state of the world and their place within it is abandoned. This is especially the case for students who are placed in "non-academic" streams on the grounds that they are concrete thinkers, good with their hands, lacking in basic skills, or whatever other label is attached to them.

Ironically, the schools at the same time proclaim the importance of developing students' talents to the full, not simply of training and socializing them into conformity and passivity. In broad terms, the schools claim to be preparing students to live fully independent lives while also exercising social responsibility: "The ultimate aim of education is to develop the abilities of the individual in order to fulfill personal aspirations while making a positive contribution to society."(Alberta, 1978, p.2) Such, at least, is the message of official statements of educational policy and philosophy. There is much in such statements that democratic socialists can support, and they can be useful tools in the struggle to improve the quality of education. The task to-day is not so much to change the goals of education, as described in official documents. Rather it is to ensure that schools take the goals seriously and put them into practice, instead of ignoring them or using them as a veneer to hide the truth of what they are actually doing. Taken at face value, the many statements of educational goals published in Canada are full of high ideals. They are often worded very generally and can thus be given a variety of interpretations, but they contain the potential for a socialist educational critique.

These goals give rise to four questions that can be asked of any given school programme or activity. Firstly, does it apply to all students equally? Secondly, does it help students to think more carefully about their own goals? Thirdly, does it help students contribute actively to the society in which they live? Fourthly, does it open questions about desirable social change?

When faced with these four questions, many programmes—especially those in which many working-class students are placed—will be found wanting. They do not live up to the ideals expressed in statements of educational philosophy. These four questions, in fact, contain the potential for radical educational reform. If we begin with them and ask how schools and curricula should seek to answer them, education might take on a shape quite different from the one that currently exists.

The examination and establishment of goals is not some arid academic exercise, but rather a vital element in the task of examining education and moving it in new directions. Goals offer a lever of influence: they describe what someone thinks education is for, and therefore can be supported or challenged accordingly. They provide a standard against which to analyse practices, to see how far schools are able to meet their own ideals. They also offer a way to practical improvement, for recent research suggests that schools are most effective when they evince a shared "ethos". In other words, when administrators, teachers, students and parents share a common vision for the school, when they generally agree on what are acceptable standards and expectations, when they work together in enforcing them, and when their everyday practice is obviously based on them, schools are happier, more effective institutions.

Educational Goals in Canada

Official statements of educational goals and philosophy show a commitment to a sort of educational liberalism in which schools are expected to meet individual needs while also serving society, and in which due acknowledgement is paid to the pursuit of knowledge and rational inquiry. Saskatchewan, for example, describes its social studies curriculum in these terms:

> Social studies education encompasses the development of desirable personal, social and civic behaviour... It should help students to think, to develop problem-solving, creative and decision-making skills, and to formulate attitudes and values for social and democratic living. In addition, it should better prepare students to deal with their problems, to accept and endeavour to improve their world and to acquire social learnings which should enable them to function as responsible and effective citizens of a democratic society. (Saskatchewan, 1983, p.47)

This Saskatchewan statement is typical of all the provinces and territories. It indicates that, while schools are for the most part conservative places, they are at the very least pledged to improve the quality of society. Thus they lay claim to fostering independent thinking, participation and a heightened sense of community. In the words of an Alberta document, they want to "help students develop intellectual independence, moral maturity and more effective involvement in the political, economic and social affairs of their communities."(Alberta, 1978) It is true that these words can be given a conservative gloss, but there is nothing inherently conservative about them. The most radical teachers could justify their practices on the grounds that they were fostering intellectual independence and moral maturity.

Across the country curriculum guidelines speak of independence or autonomy, envisaging ideal citizens as those who have the skills and the ability to support themselves financially. Beyond this kind of *economic* independence, the guidelines also speak of *intellectual* autonomy, of citizens who can make up their own minds, who are not easily swayed or manipulated by others, who follow the dictates of both reason and conscience. Added to these two kinds of autonomy is a third, which might best be described as *psychological.* This envisages the ideal citizen as someone who lives a healthy, balanced life, who finds adequate outlets for energies and interests, who has, so to speak, come to terms with himself or herself, who has had the opportunity to explore a wide range of interests.

Curriculum guidelines also say a great deal about participation and involvement. They see the ideal citizen as someone who is knowledgeable about and involved in the local community and in wider provincial and national affairs. As far back as 1897, the Winnipeg School Board spoke of the importance of schools in laying "the foundation for intelligent participation in public affairs," and this idea has become increasingly popular over the years, to the point that some schools are now encouraged not just to lay the foundation for later participation, but actually to get students directly involved in public affairs while they are still in school. The Manitoba social studies programme, for example, lists the usual objectives of knowledge, values and skills but also adds a "social participation" category. Most of the participation objectives remain within the classroom walls, promoting such activities as group-work, helping other students and so on, but there is explicit mention of "participating in volunteer work that helps the elderly, young children, ill, handicapped; participating in or observing efforts directed towards solving some community problems; criticizing society constructively and working to improve it where necessary; participating in a political campaign of a candidate of the student's own choice, etc." (Manitoba, 1981, p.3) Most provinces do not go this far, although in almost any school district one can find teachers who involve their students in such activities no matter what the curriculum says. British Columbia, for example, speaks specifically of "citizenship skills," but restricts them to in-school settings, with the skills being defined as "self-worth, interpersonal relations, group and discussion skills, and leadership." Alberta lists what it calls "participation skills," but these also are restricted to classroom activities.

This emphasis on participation and involvement has led schools to address themselves explicitly to matters of skills and values. These are, of course, questions that have concerned schools from the very beginning, but in recent years they have received a new emphasis. On the one side are those who argue that society is changing so rapidly that most knowledge quickly becomes obsolete, so that it is important to teach students the skills needed to cope with an uncertain future. On the other side are those who believe in the importance of a more or less fixed body of knowledge and skills that will help people cope with change and uncertainty, not least by providing some fixed standards to protect them from drift and confusion. In reality, the appropriate course does not lie in choosing one or the other, but rather in a proper balance between the two, and this is the context that has led school curricula to say more and more about skills, often including elaborate grids and charts identifying skills in minute detail and using them to plot students' progress from grade to grade.

In broad terms, schools see the good citizen as having mastered at least three types of skills: one, the traditional academic skills of communication, research and critical thinking; two, the behavioural skills that are necessary for successful participation and involvement, whether in school or society; and, three, what are usually called social or interpersonal skills. There is nothing to be said in elaboration of the first. The three R's, the ability to pursue a research project, to think in a rational, organized way, are all perfectly familiar. Nor is there any need to say more about the second, for it is obvious that if students are to be involved in the life of the school and even of the wider society, they must acquire the skills needed to do so; and there is nothing very complicated about the definition of these skills, although it is much more difficult to teach them than to define them. Discussion, persuasion, analysis, action, working with others, organization—these are the fundamentals. The third category—interpersonal and social skills—are also not particularly difficult to identify and define, but it is worth keeping in mind that they have become an important concern of the schools.

Taken at their face value, statements of educational goals and specifications of curriculum frequently stress co-operation and working together. They are insistent upon the importance of students living and working together without friction and upon the idea that the school is a community in which everyone should play a part. Words, however, are slippery things, and the rhetoric of community and co-operation can be used to cover a wide variety of motives. Nonetheless, it would be wrong to ignore the importance that teachers and educational leaders have attached to the co-operative spirit. Thus, for example, in connection with the Empire Day festivities of 1899, the Ontario Department of Education worried lest its encouragement of patriotic and Empire spirit might lead to chauvinism and aggression. It called for "a patriotism inspired by a higher conception of civic duty, improved devotion to the public interest, willingness to offer personal service on behalf of one another, and a disposition to give assistance for the promotion of social improvement.""(Chaiton & McDonald, 1977, p.105) Indeed, it was precisely the existence of conflict and competition that made schools so important, for many of those who supported compulsory education in the nineteenth and early twentieth centuries did so in the hope that schools would reduce the divisiveness that they feared was threatening the social fabric. Schools have long held to the tradition of advocating social consensus and deprecating conflict. Egerton Ryerson put it this way in the 1840's: "All arbitrary class distinctions, professional exclusiveness and hostile factions are, then, so many impediments to the social advancement of the country; and as they prevail to a less or greater extent, will the energies of society for the common welfare be crippled and paralyzed?""(McDonald & Chaiton, 1978, p.96) Thus, it was important to get children to attend a common school and to learn their proper lessons, in order to encourage "the spirit of true patriotism by making each now feel that the welfare of the whole society is his welfare—that collective interests are first in order of importance and duty, and separate interests are second."

There is obviously a strong conservative streak in this kind of thinking, reminiscent of the classic manœuvre by which people are persuaded to set aside particular interests of class, group or region in favour of an alleged greater national good. The argument clearly favours the privileged at the expense of those less privileged by aiming to persuade those with grievances to put them aside and work together. In this regard, the schools' emphasis on consensus and co-operation can be an instrument of class interest, working to protect those with power and influence against those without.

At the same time, it has to be realized that there is also a strong element in educational thought, especially in Canada, that sees co-operation as good in itself, regardless of context. This, no doubt, derives in part from the Christian background of many early educators, fully imbued with the spirit of neighbourly love and the principles of the Sermon of the Mount. In more modern form, it reveals itself not so much in any religious impulse, but in a generalized feeling among many teachers that society could be a much better place than it is. Although we know very little about the social or political philosophy of Canadian teachers, it is hard to escape the impression that many of them subscribe to what might be termed a helping ethic, and share a conviction that education is the key to individual and social improvement, even if this is often expressed in remarkably a-political terms. Usually, society is seen as an undifferentiated whole with certain needs and aspirations, so that the role and influence of particular groups is obscured.

There is a long history in educational discussion of phrases such as "society wants," "the needs of society," "society expects," all of which imply that there is such a thing as society, whose needs, interests and expectations are easily identified. One finds this, for example, in the classic formulation of Emile Durkheim, the pioneer French sociologist, who defined education as

> The influence exercised by adult generations on those that are not yet ready for social life. Its object is to arouse and develop in the child a certain number of physical, intellectual and moral states which are required of him both by the political society as a whole and by the special milieu for which he is specially destined.(Lukes, 1972, p.132)

This kind of definition ignores the divisions that exist within a society, by speaking of "society as a whole," and thus ignores the fact that some groups in society have the power to make decisions about the education of others. However, Durkheim's definition describes the viewpoint of many teachers, who see themselves rather as the agents (and sometimes the victims) of society as a whole. It is not difficult to find this point of view embedded in curricula, as demonstrated in this Grade 5 Saskatchewan example:

> Students will also learn how Canadians have used regional differences to develop a spirit of co-operation, interdependence and common goals which are reflected in unifying symbols such as the flag, the national anthem, a central government and an east/west communication system.(Saskatchewan, 1983)

This seems rather an optimistic view of the role of regional differences in Canadian history and politics, even at the Grade 5 level, but it is not uncommon in curricula and it does illustrate how the values of co-operation and consensus, together with the skills involved in interpersonal and social relationships, inform curriculum.

This example also shows the important role that values play in school curricula and programmes. Some conservative critics of the schools accuse them of becoming utterly relative and situational, and of preaching the moral code that anything goes. While it is true that schools no longer purvey the moral certainties that they did two or three generations ago, and are much more sensitive to the dangers of indoctrination, especially in a country that officially espouses diversity, this criticism is fundamentally mistaken. Some schools have experimented with approaches that encourage students to question accepted values and to formulate their own value systems, but one does not have to look far to find fundamental values virtually leaping from the pages of curriculum documents. Manitoba speaks of developing in students "an appreciation of and positive attitudes towards the diverse cultures to be found in the local, national and international social environments," and emphasizes "concern for the well-being and dignity of others," "positive ways of dealing with prejudices, discrimination and stereotyping," as well as "an appreciation for such procedural values as respect for truth, freedom, toleration, fairness and respect for reasoning." (Manitoba, 1981, pp.1-3) Alberta pulls no punches and says that "within the secondary school context, the development of desirable personal characteristics such as integrity, honesty, fairness, generosity, self-esteem, respect for others, responsibility for one's actions, a sense of justice, tolerance, open-mindedness, respect for the environment, sharing, stewardship, and cooperation should be fostered."(Alberta, 1985, p.17) Similar statements are easily found in all the provinces and territories and it is clear what the stated values of the school system are. They can be identified, in general terms, as hard work, tolerance, co-operation, moderation, rationality, fair-play, a sense of justice, and social participation.

Add to this a moderate patriotism, and we have the schools' definition of the good citizen. It is, on the surface, an acceptable and, indeed, attractive picture. If we were to judge the schools purely in terms of their goals and ideals, there would be little to criticize. Indeed, if they had been able to achieve their goals, Canadian society could be quite different. The problem lies not in what the schools say they would like to accomplish, but rather in the obstacles that impede progress towards that end. Classrooms have for the most part continued to be conservative places, in which the emphasis is upon order and control. As a result what students are supposed to learn is contradicted by the concrete reality of their classroom experience. This arises largely from the nature of teachers' working conditions, but it is secured by the general ignorance—amongst teachers, students and parents—of their school system's goals. It is as if educational goals are formulated as a ritual quite distinct from the real work of developing actual programmes, selecting textbooks, training teachers, and classroom teaching. Consequently they have little connection with the day-to-day world of schools. As a result, the good citizen that actually emerges from the classrooms bears only passing resemblance to the image contained in statements of educational philosophy. The task, then, is one of turning these philosophical statements into reality. The problem lies not with the goals as such, but with their implementation.

A Democratic Socialist Curriculum

In recent years, socialists and others on the left have been more successful in criticizing the schools than in suggesting how they should change. As necessary as such analysis is, and as useful as it can be in demystifying current practice, it is of only limited use if it does not lead to positive action. Unfortunately, it has too often led to the conclusion that such action is either impossible or useless, for, if the schools are indeed the instruments—or perhaps the prisoners—of the ruling class, it is unlikely that they will be allowed to turn against their controllers.

In reality, schools enjoy a certain amount of freedom of action, often more than is commonly supposed, the limits of which can be defined only by testing them. Teachers are not the captives of some ideological wire-puller: they can draw upon the traditional concept of liberal education, which places a high priority on the value of independent thought. And, as I have tried to make clear, there is much in existing statements of educational goals and philosophies that can be used to make sure that schools live up to their potential.

This is not the place to offer a detailed prescription for a democratic socialist approach to curriculum. The conception of socialism from which this book arises values local action and initiatives in dealing with community problems. It emphasizes emancipation, empowerment and participation, rather than the alleged efficiencies of centralized planning and direction. In this context, there can be no centrally planned and mandated curriculum destined to fit all schools in all circumstances. Rather, teachers, students, parents and the community at large must work together to develop curricula that will be both educationally worthwhile and appropriate to the particular circumstances of the students for whom they are intended. Thus, for example, the New Zealand Ministry of Education in 1984 recommended that schools should develop their own curricula through consultation with the communities in which they are located and within a broad framework of national criteria. These New Zealand criteria have much to say to anyone interested in thinking through questions of curriculum. In essence, they are as follows:

1. The curriculum must be common for all students and schools.
2. The curriculum must be accessible to all students, regardless of gender, class, race, ethnic background, or alleged ability and aptitude.
3. The curriculum must be non-racist.
4. The curriculum must be non-sexist.
5. The curriculum must be designed so that all students enjoy significant success.
6. The curriculum should reflect the need to make education a life-long process, especially through helping

students learn how to learn.

7. The curriculum must be seen as a totality, not simply a collection of isolated subjects and experiences.
8. The curriculum must be broad and general, rather than narrowly vocational.
9. The curriculum for every student must be of the highest quality.
10. The curriculum must be planned so that all its components are consistent and serve the intended goals.
11. The curriculum must be cooperatively designed by those who comprise the school and its community.
12. The curriculum must be continually reviewed by those who designed it in order to ensure that it is both worthwhile and appropriate.
13. The curriculum must be user-friendly and must not exclude or alienate students.
14. The curriculum must be aimed at empowering students to take control over their own lives.
15. The curriculum must ensure that students enjoy learning. (New Zealand, 1987, pp.10-11)

These criteria have most to say about how curricula should be planned, implemented and taught. They specify what a curriculum must do, without prescribing how it must be done. This same approach can equally be applied to the contents of the curriculum, where a set of broad criteria can be established, within which curriculum-planning groups can work. Such a framework for a democratic socialist approach to curriculum might well look like the following, which is not intended to be accepted as it stands, but rather to serve as an entry-point into the debate over what educational goals the schools should be striving to achieve.

1. *Academic/Intellectual Goals*

(i) Knowledge and experience of languages and literature; mathematics and science; humanities and social science; expressive arts; practical arts
(ii) Basic skills

    (iii) Research skills
    (iv)   Rational thinking
    (v)   Creativity
    (vi)   Commitment to further learning

2. *Citizenship Goals*

    (i)   Knowledge of Canada and the world
    (ii)   Familiarity with current affairs
    (iii) Political literacy
    (iv)   Commitment to internationalism and peace
    (v)   Commitment to social equality and justice
    (vi)   Commitment to environmental principles ˙
    (vii) Knowledge of both official languages
    (viii) Skills and dispositions appropriate to political/social
           participation
    (ix)   Experience in community service

3. *Interpersonal goals*

    (i)   Tolerance of and respect for others, with special
           emphasis on multiculturalism, anti-racism and anti-
           sexism
    (ii)   Belief in and commitment to cooperation

4. *Personal Development Goals*

    (i)   Physical health and fitness
    (ii)   Emotional balance
    (iii) Positive and balanced self-image
    (iv)   Life skills

5. *Moral Goals*

    (i)   Commitment to moral principles
    (ii)   Sense of conscience and social obligation

6. *Vocational Goals*

    (i)   Work habits and skills
    (ii)   Ability to plan and organize

This list is necessarily general. It does not, for example, specify what the moral principles are, or what is involved in acquiring work habits and skills, or how much knowledge of literature or science is sufficient, and so on. What is intended is not a detailed blueprint but rather a set of categories that can be used to investigate statements of educational goals, to provide a basis for the development of such statements where they do not exist and, above all, to provide some framework for discussion about what schools should be trying to accomplish, though many of the goals listed here are obviously not the sole responsibility of the school.

    Perhaps the most distinctive features of such a democratic socialist approach to curriculum are these. First, *all* students, not just those who are thought to be "academic" in orientation, must be exposed to the fullest range of human knowledge. Second, this knowledge is not an end in itself, but is important for the light it sheds both on current concerns and the persisting human issues and for its ability to enrich and empower students. Third, the curriculum is to embody the values of cooperation, justice, freedom, equality, community and empowerment: it is directed to the development of active, socially committed citizens, not passive spectators or armchair theorists. Fourth, knowledge and action must be linked so that students learn how to refine, extend and apply their knowledge through action in the real world. In this regard, it is important that, as an integral part of the curriculum, students be involved in some form of community service.

Community Involvement and Service

    The need to be active, to make an impact, to be empowered, appears time and again when adolescent students are allowed to speak freely, and teachers often sense it. In Manitoba, for example, a 1984 survey organized by the Manitoba Teachers Society reported that "student apathy and lack of motivation are perceived to be major concerns," with students suffering from "feelings of hopelessness."

The survey linked this student mood with worries about unemployment and the possibility of nuclear war, and there is no doubt something to this, but it is equally possible that students were reacting to a generalized sense of powerlessness and uselessness. This came out clearly at a 1985 Winnipeg Seminar on Youth and The Law, at which students over-whelmingly complained of "frustration that their opinions are not taken seriously" and argued that "they should have a greater part in making decisions that affect them."(*Winnipeg Free Press*, Dec. 10, 1984 and Nov. 13, 1985)

In the conditions of modern technological society, schools have cut children off from the world of which they are a part and, with the best of intentions, denied them any possibility of making any meaningful contribution to society. Ironically, at the very time when young people are for the most part bigger, stronger and better nourished than ever before, and when they are achieving physical maturity at an earlier age, they have to wait longer and longer to be regarded as adults. It is true that the voting age has been lowered and that the age of eighteen has acquired some of the symbolism that used to be attached to the age of twenty-one, but the years from approximately fourteen to eighteen have become a wasteland. They are a period of high energy and idealism, but we have effectively denied teenagers any chance of playing a useful or valued role in society; condemning them instead, to a life of waiting and triviality, on the grounds that they are not yet mature. The words of the U.S. psychologist, Urie Bronfenbrenner, are worth pondering:

> Our children are not entrusted with any real responsi-
> bilities; the ends and means have been determined by
> someone else and their job is to fulfil an assignment
> involving little judgement, decision-making or risk.
> This practice is intended to protect children from
> burdens beyond their years, but there is reason to
> believe it had been carried too far. (Bronfenbrenner,
> 1974, p.60)

These words are clearly applicable to schools and indeed to most of the part-time jobs that so many teenagers now hold, for these jobs are usually tightly planned and controlled, with prescribed behaviour spelled out, and little or no room for individual initiative. Such jobs, whatever their merits in giving teenagers some spending money of their own and hence a certain independence, serve to reinforce the view that work is simply something to be done to earn money to spend on the really important things in life. And these things are themselves often the creation of the mass media or the entertainment industry, which have done much to foster and to profit from the existence of a separate youth culture. It is not surprising that Bibby and Posterski conclude from their national survey of Canadian youth that "Adults have set teenagers up for disenchantment and disappointment... Stated simply, the problem is the failure of adults to let young people grow up. Expressed another way, adults suppress emergence." (Bibby & Posterski, 1985, p.4)

We are not helping our students if we deny them the chance for involvement, for practical action. This certainly is one of the messages of Don Sawyer's experience of teaching in a small Newfoundland outport, where he found that it was possible to reach youngsters who were disillusioned, unmotivated and apathetic (at least so far as school was concerned) by involving them actively in their own learning in ways and on topics that made sense to them, rather than sitting them down and making them follow the prescribed curriculum. Education should enable young people to make a genuine contribution to society, and it should establish real links between school and the outside world.

There are many reasons why this is important but the three most important have to do with the related concepts of community, participation and empowerment. It is a truism to say that contemporary conditions have eroded people's sense of community. Whether one speaks of individualism, of Christopher Lasch's concept of narcissism, of Galbraith's contrast between private wealth and public squalor, it is clear that individual self-interest has become the measure of modern living. Profit and privatization are highly prized, service and the public good are devalued. At the same time, the increasing size and complexity of institutions make them more remote and impersonal. What is lost in all this is a sense of belonging, a sense of social responsibility and of social living, so that the guiding principles become "What's in it for me?" and "Let's make a deal." Education has also come to be dominated by what Hargreaves calls the "culture of individualism", with much attention being given to what are thought to be the needs of students but little to the kind of society that education could help to produce. What students learn is to think, not in terms of the community or the social good, but in terms of their individual interest.

In one sense, this argument can be given a very conservative reading so that it becomes a prolonged indictment of the corrosive impact of modern technology and a lament for some mythical past, when there were standards and values, and people knew their place. The concept of community can be and has been used by conservatives as much as by radicals. However, the conservative view collapses when the concept of community is enriched with the further concepts of participation and empowerment. What is envisaged here is not some hierarchical order in which people carry out their allotted responsibilities and do not speak out of turn, but rather a society in which there is the highest degree of participation at all levels and in which people feel entitled, equipped and empowered to participate. This is manifestly not the case today where most people feel that things are out of control, or that they cannot make a difference, and where institutions are organized not so much to encourage participation but rather to provide only for representation. There are good reasons for us to speak of "representative" democracy and in to-day's world it is not to be despised. The task is not to destroy it or dismantle it, but to preserve its virtues and go beyond it to a democracy which assumes participation. The aim is to breathe new life into the long-established but too easily forgotten Canadian tradition of the co-operative commonwealth, a society in which all co-operate for the common well-being of everyone.

Schools, unwittingly, often work against this and produce not socially conscious, participating and empowered citizens, but rather the reverse. It is not unrealistic to think that schools can counter this process and that to include an element of community service in the curriculum is one way to achieve it.

It must be stressed that this is not simply one more item to be added to the existing curriculum, nor a distraction from the academic "basics," but rather a vital part of a new approach to curriculum and an important educational experience both in its own right and in the links that can be established with other subjects.

Its advantages are obvious. In the first place, it helps to give students a sense of community and the skills and dispositions upon which participation depends, and so benefits both the students and the community. Secondly, it helps to provide a sense of empowerment, of what Newmann calls "environmental competence." Thirdly, it reduces the sense of sterility and isolation that so often pervades the school curriculum today. Fourthly, it can help to provide the sense of motivation and purpose in students that teachers say is so often missing today. In this regard, it is worth noting that, at present, work-experience programmes are generally seen as a way of coping with students' aversion to school. Fifthly, it will help the young themselves, for when adolescents are not allowed to exercise any meaningful responsibility, they will find maturity more difficult to achieve.

There is already in existence a small but growing trend, especially in the area of political and social education, to involve students in planned, educationally worthwhile out-of-school experiences, and especially to get them involved in community affairs. Such activities can take many forms, including:

- Planning and developing bicycle trails
- Organizing a campaign for community sports facilities
- Conducting surveys
- Working in political campaigns
- Engaging in political action on specific issues
- Working in hospitals, nursing homes and other institutions
- Preparing and presenting briefs to the local council
- Taking action on traffic, pollution or other community problems

And to this list of examples, one could add those schools that require their students to work with younger children or with old people, and that involve them in community action projects and wider political issues.

Such an approach goes far beyond simple community work, for it must also include an important educational component. It engages students in making choices and establishing priorities for action; it demands much planning and organization; it necessitates considerable research into problems; it often confronts political realities; it provides a basis for analysis, thought and discussion. Conrad and Hedin suggest five criteria for assessing the value of projects that include community service and involvement:

1. students should have some responsibility for making their own decisions;
2. they should have other people depend on their actions;
3. they should work on tasks that extend their thinking, both cognitively and ethically;
4. they should work with age groups other than their own;

5. they should reflect systematically on their experience.
(Conrad & Hedin, 1977, pp.134-5)

In other words, any community service experience that is educationally worthwhile must pay attention to the educational values it is intended to serve. Action for its own sake is not enough; it must both arise from and lead to reflection upon knowledge.

Chapter 3

A Working-Class Curriculum

Class and Learning

Students from different social class backgrounds are being taught different things. Sometimes this is deliberate, for it is clear that, where programmes are divided into academic and vocational tracks (or whatever particular system is applied), working-class students are over-represented in the less academic programmes. Such programmes are intended to provide a level of difficulty appropriate to a student's alleged aptitude, without being either too easy and thus conferring no educational benefit, or too difficult and thus humiliating the student unnecessarily. Despite this, it is hard to avoid the impression that the less academic courses often become a dumping-ground, so that neither teachers nor students themselves seriously try to tackle problems that they judge too difficult. Instead, the curriculum is adjusted downwards to what it is thought the students can do. Too often one hears teachers chide classes with such admonitions as, "Come on, you're acting like general course kids," or "I thought you were supposed to be the university entrance class." Indeed, students themselves adopt this way of thinking, rejecting this or that assignment with the argument, "We're not university entrance, you know." In short, expectations are lowered and the self-fulfilling prophecy quickly takes effect: these are judged to be "non-academic" students (whatever that may mean), they are taught accordingly, and they begin to act according to expectations, and soon define themselves in these same terms.

Despite the technical criticism levelled against it, Rosenthal's research on the "Pygmalion effect," suggesting that students' success or failure in school may be a reflection of their teachers' judgments and expectations rather than of any innate ability, carries a ring of truth. It is easy to see how, in time, students will respond to all those indications by which teachers, either knowingly or unwittingly, reveal their judgments of them—judgments often, though mistakenly, thought to have an objective, scientific base, in I.Q. and other tests, in records of previous work, and so on. In a similar vein, in his study of kindergarten and the early elementary grades, Rist showed how students sorted themselves out according to the attention and responses given them by their teachers, responses based far more often upon the social status, respectability, and co-operation of the children than upon their ability or intelligence.

There is also an increasing amount of research that shows that academic classes are taught differently from general or vocational classes. In academic classes, in which the students generally co-operate with their teachers and accept the educational standards and expectations of the schools, the emphasis is placed upon a certain level of independence, questioning, and thinking for oneself. In vocational or general classes, by contrast, lower-order tasks are emphasized, with more frequent use of exercises, of fill-in-the-blank worksheets, of obeying instructions and following orders. It is a perfect reflection of and preparation for the division in society at large between those who make decisions and issue instructions and those whose task it is simply to follow them.

It should be emphasized that this is not simply a judgment that teachers impose on pupils regardless of the evidence. On the contrary, it is in many ways a rational assessment, for so-called less academic students do not share their teachers' evaluations of what is important, nor do they disguise their real feelings, as their more academic counterparts might. Nell Keddie found little difference between A stream and C stream students' understanding of the material they were studying. The difference between them lay more in their outward reactions and the teachers' assessments of them. Her conclusion is striking, for she argued that it might well be academic students' willingness to play the school game and thus not to challenge the curriculum or their teachers that leads teachers to look kindly upon them, which in turn encourages the students to co-operate more, and so on. In Keddie's words, "It would seem to be the failure of high-ability pupils to question what they are taught in schools that contributes in large measure to their educational achievement."(Young, 1971, pp. 134 ff.) Indeed, this suggestion is consistent with the experience of some teachers that the best discussions often occur with so-called less academic students, who feel they have nothing to lose, rather than with the best and the brightest, who are often obsessed with what is going to be on the test. It is also consistent with Hodgett's finding, in *What Culture? What Heritage?*, that the best lessons he observed took place at all levels of the school and were not confined only to the most academic students.

Working-Class Students and the Academic Curriculum

Nonetheless, this has not prevented some commentators from concluding that the "academic" curriculum is not suitable for many students, especially those from the working class. This argument comes in at least three variants that can be conveniently called élitist, liberal, and relativist.

The élitist view holds that only a minority of people at any age-level are capable of understanding those matters that should be central to the academic curriculum and that can for convenience be described as high culture. This view has been most bluntly stated by literary critics such as F.R. Leavis and T.S. Eliot:

> It is impossible to question the clear fact: only a minority is capable of advanced intellectual culture...
> It is disastrous to let a country's educational arrangements be determined, or even be affected, by the assumption that a high intellectual standard can be attained by more than an overall minority. (Entwhistle, 1978, p.136)

The obvious educational implication of this view is that most students, and by definition most working-class students, are incapable of understanding an intellectually oriented curriculum, and therefore must do something else in its place.

The liberal view is more cautious, holding not that most students are necessarily incapable of advanced intellectual work, but that the conventional school curriculum is not the best way to achieve it. The liberal argument rests on fact—that many students are bored by the conventional curriculum—and partly on assumption—that the conventional curriculum unfairly penalizes too many students, especially if they are from a working-class background. This view has been nicely stated by Hargreaves: "The more profound and more disturbing message is that the very concept of ability becomes closely tied to the intellectual-cognitive domain. 'Intelligence' becomes defined as the ability to master the cognitive-intellectual aspects of school subjects." This leads to schools having to compel students to study things in which they are not interested, with a resultant emphasis on control and discipline rather than learning, to the mutual loss of both teachers and students who thus find themselves trapped in a cycle of move and counter-move that makes the classroom more like a battleground than a centre of learning. Hargreaves concludes: "My argument is that our present secondary school system, largely through the hidden curriculum, exerts on many pupils, particularly but by no means exclusively from the working class, a destruction of their dignity which is so massive and pervasive that few subsequently recover from it."(Hargreaves, 1982, pp. 17 and 61)

The major objection to this and other versions of the same argument is that the problem does not lie in the emphasis on the "intellectual-cognitive" but rather in the way it is embedded in a particular constellation of school subjects, organized and taught in certain ways. It is not that students, whether working-class or not, cannot handle intellectual-cognitive work. This is not what they dislike. What they object to is particular subject-matter, taught in certain ways. And it should be stressed that for the most part there is nothing very intellectually demanding about most school subjects, for the evidence is that in most cases emphasis is placed not upon sophisticated intellectual operations but upon memory work, worksheets, and related drudgery. It was precisely this that Don Sawyer found in his Newfoundland outport school and that was stopping his students dead in their educational tracks. His solution, like that of many of our best teachers, was not to abandon intellectual work but to find new ways of approaching it that combined much of the traditional content with students' personal experience.

The relativist view shares with the liberal position the belief that the academic curriculum is irrelevant to large numbers of students but it goes much further by regarding all knowledge as arbitrary and therefore rejects all claims that some kinds of knowledge are somehow "better" than others. It is a view usually described as radical, because it asks fundamental questions about school curricula and because it tends to be associated with radical political views. However, it is not shared by all those with radical views and to describe it as radical excludes other approaches with equal claims to the title. It seems reasonable, therefore, to follow Brian Simon's example and call it "relativist".

The relativists see the academic curriculum as an ideological imposition by one class upon another. This curriculum, they argue, is at one and the same time a way of discrediting and delegitimizing working-class culture and experience by refusing to include them in the curriculum, thus denying their claim to worthwhile status, while also imposing upon the working class, in the guise of educational standards and academic integrity, a view of the world that is not only not theirs but that is actually hostile to their interests. The implication of this point of view is that the curriculum should reflect the values and priorities of working-class culture rather than those of "high-culture", which is, in fact, only bourgeois culture in disguise and which is irrelevant to most working-class students who have, in any case, rejected it.

This view has been criticized by some on the left as not being really radical at all in any meaningful political sense (hence Simon's term, "relativist"). It is, says Simon, "a new ideological means of denying to the working class access to knowledge, culture and science." Furthermore, he says, it is "an unbelievably a-historical (and entirely speculative) theory..." that would only serve to ghettoize working-class students and thus confirm them in their subordinate status. (Simon, 1976, pp. 171-2) If working-class students have not taken to the traditional curriculum, the solution is not to abandon it totally, but to find ways of organizing and teaching it, so that they can take possession of it for themselves. This view does not deny that the traditional curriculum is ideologically biased, but it separates knowledge as such from the way it is used ideologically. To take a specific example: classical music should not be eliminated from the curriculum on the grounds that it is an alien intrusion upon working-class culture; rather, it should be incorporated in an approach that sees music as an indispensable and valuable form of human expression which can take many forms, including not only the classical, but also jazz, folk, pop, rock and so on. At the same time, the labelling of different kinds of music should be investigated: what does it mean to call a particular form of music "classical." What are the implications of the word? What social purposes are served? Who does the labelling? Can and should other forms of music properly be called "classical"? In music as in other subjects, the task is to lead students to see the world as it is, to ask questions they otherwise might not have asked, to reconsider their own and others' unchallenged assumptions, to consider alternatives and to shape their lives accordingly. And none of this is possible if students are not introduced to the richness of human experience, past and present. We are not helping working-class students if we deny them this on the grounds that it is an ideological imposition or devalues their own cultural experience or is simply too difficult for them.

Working-class curriculum

There can be no doubt that existing curricula are biased, both in what they include and in what they omit; nor that for many working-class students they have little interest or appeal, though in this regard the picture is more complex than some critics suggest. It is clear also that schools have been intended to serve as instruments of the dominant ideology, playing their part in reproducing the social order and maintaining cultural hegemony, though they nonetheless enjoy a certain level of independence. In this context, some theorists have advanced the concept of a working-class curriculum, arguing that the existing curriculum is undemocratic because it is a form of ideological domination and because it denies working-class students a true education, either by blinding them to their real situation or by diverting them from any chance of educational success. This class-biased process is strengthened by the very success of those working-class students who do "make it," since this both obscures what is really happening by making it appear fair and open, and by stripping the working class of its potential leaders. Thus, it is argued, there should be a working-class curriculum that would address only working-class concerns, draw only upon working-class culture, and offer only working-class students a genuinely relevant and emancipatory education.

This is the "relativist" position and can be contrasted with another which will be described here as "democratic socialist" and to which we shall return shortly. The latter argues that, in the broadest sense, the form and content of traditional school curriculum are not all wrong, and much of it must be retained and strengthened. It needs of course constant revision, particularly in exposing and changing its ideological and political bias, but we should be careful not to throw out the baby with the bathwater. The traditional curriculum that has grown up in our schools is not simply the product of ruling-class demands, but has also been constructed by teachers and farmers, workers and professionals, who wanted the truth to be told and society changed for the better. The task is not to design a new working-class curriculum, but rather to make the existing curriculum serve a genuinely educational function by fulfilling the promise contained in its own statements of goals.

It is not altogether clear what the "relativist" concept of a working-class curriculum entails in practice. In general terms, it is clearly intended to be a curriculum that working-class students will find interesting and relevant to their own experience, that will give them the skills, insights and knowledge to enable them to take control of their lives, and that will play its part in producing desirable social change. More specifically, such a curriculum is intended for working-class students and draws upon working-class culture and experience, although it should be noted that the two notions are not necessarily identical. For example, one can envisage a curriculum that says a lot about working-class life and culture but that is studied by middle-class students, in the same way that anthropologists study a culture without being members of it. Indeed, one might argue that the very people who should know more about the texture of working-class life are those middle-class teachers, social workers, bureaucrats and other social engineers who are so busily intervening in it, though usually from the outside. There is a touch of arrogance in the assumption that middle-class teachers are going to enlighten working-class students about the realities of their lives. And there is something self-defeating about the assumption that working-class students find most "relevant" only that which relates directly to their daily concerns. One only has to hear their conversations, check their television and film watching, listen to their music, look at their reading, to realize very quickly that working-class students have as rich and vivid an imagination as anyone else. It is difficult to see why anyone should think that they would find a community problem more interesting than, say, science-fiction, space travel, or the private life of Henry VIII.

There is, in fact, a thorny practical problem facing any attempt to design a working-class curriculum in either of the two senses just described. If it is intended for working-class students, the first challenge is to decide which students these are. If it is to draw upon working-class culture and experience, then we have to be able to identify these with some precision in order to make the development of a curriculum possible, especially at a time when working-class culture has been so penetrated by the mass-media and by other cultural forms. Working-

39

class culture, like any other, is not a single, undifferentiated entity and it is by no means certain which elements of it, or whose interpretations of it, should be embodied in a curriculum.

The community-based curriculum

The most common solution to this problem has been to root working-class education in the characteristics and concerns of the local community, as was done in the Educational Priority Areas (EPA's) that were created in Britain in the 1970's:

> If we are concerned with the majority of children who will spend their lives in EPA's, rather than only with the minority who will leave them for universities and colleges and middle-class occupations elsewhere, then the schools must set out to equip their children to meet the grim reality of the social environment in which they live and reform it in all its aspects... Only if they are armed with intimate familiarity with their immediate problems may they be expected to articulate the needs they feel and create the means for satisfying them. The obvious danger here is that of creating a second-class education for second-class citizens through curricula restricted to local horizons. But what we intend is the opposite of a soporific: it is not to fit children for their station in life in an ascriptive sense. It is to accept that many children must live out their lives in deprived areas and to inspire them to think boldly about it rather than lapse into resigned apathy. (Halsey, 1972, p..114)

Despite this acknowledgement of the dangers of creating a second-class education, it cannot be said that this approach avoids them. It is, admittedly, not clear what is involved in "thinking boldly" about living in a deprived area, and no one can object to anything that reduces or eliminates "resigned apathy," but a community-based curriculum is not necessarily the best or the only means to do this. And certainly not if it is intended to apply *only* to working-class students. It is certainly desirable for schools to deal with problems and issues that their students see as real, but there are many possibilities for this in the existing curriculum which could, if they were used, serve the combined purpose of addressing the "real world" while at the same time introducing students to a wider and deeper range of human knowledge. It does not take much imagination to see that subjects such as history, social studies, literature, home economics and science can easily embrace "real world" issues. Moving from the students' own experiences and interests to broader educational and social concerns is a matter more of pedagogy than content. This does not mean that there is some magical way of stuffing, say, ancient history down unwilling throats, and there will certainly be occasions when the existing curriculum has to be thrown out and replaced by something that students find more appealing, but the answer is to be found not in restricting oneself to the local community, but in seeking out topics and materials that students will find interesting and that also introduce them to the range of human knowledge, while at the same time giving them necessary skills. Most subjects that exist in the curriculum at present are flexible enough and broad enough to make this possible.

David Hargreaves has rejected the idea that the community alone provides the best resource for a purely working-class curriculum, and has argued instead that the curriculum should be based on a combination of community-studies and expressive arts, for up to 50% of the total school-time available between the ages of eleven and fifteen, with the other 50% being devoted to remedial work in particular areas where students need it and to the pursuit of special projects in which students have a particular interest or ability. His combination of community studies and expressive arts is intended not so much to replace the existing content of the curriculum as to provide a means of reorganizing it in order to keep what is valuable and to get rid of the rest. Hargreaves' particular concern is that the traditional curriculum places too high a value on "cognitive-intellectual" tasks and thus unnecessarily penalizes students who have no interest in or aptitude for them: "We can no longer afford an education system that for too many pupils is an unpleasant induction into the experience of failure and inferiority." (Hargreaves, 1982, p.161)

This is quite true and yet doubts remain. The traditional curriculum, for example, may be meant to serve a "cognitive-intellectual" purpose, but this is not the case in practice, since it rarely goes beyond the tasks of copying, repeating and memorizing. Studies have repeatedly shown that classrooms are not, for the most part, intellectually exciting or demanding places. It seems, therefore, more likely that students are rejecting not the "cognitive-intellectual," for they get little experience of it, but rather a set of topics and subjects, and a way of approaching them, which they see little point in taking and find extremely boring. The real problem is that the "cognitive-intellectual" is too often divorced from the experiential, so that in the classroom it becomes largely a question of seat-work, memorization and teacher-organized discussion. One only has to listen to the conversation of students to realize that they demonstrate considerable cognitive-intellectual sophistication. As Labov has shown in his investigation of the speech of inner-city black Americans, underneath the bad grammar, the word play and the slang, which so often offend middle-class ears, there is an impressive amount of thinking at work. Thus, the priority is not to reject the "academic" curriculum as somehow irrelevant or harmful to students, but to find ways of connecting it with students' experience, of reshaping it when necessary, and above all seeking to involve students actively in curriculum.

A Divided Curriculum

The argument that many students, and especially those from the working class, find the curriculum uncongenial because it is too academic and intellectual, finds much support from a certain kind of conservative theory, of which the most eloquent and forthright exponent is the English educational theorist, G.H. Bantock. Bantock accepts the views of F.R. Leavis, T.S. Eliot and others that education, properly so-called, as an initiation into high culture, is achievable only for that minority in any society blessed with the refinement, the sensibility and the intellect to grasp it. In this view, any attempt to bring academic education to all students inevitably results in a lowering of standards, since most students cannot handle it, and indeed damages students themselves by leading them to frustration and failure. This will be especially the case where students are "children of low achievement, probably though not invariably of low I.Q., come from culturally deprived homes, wish to leave school as soon as possible, and find themselves employed on leaving in unskilled or semi-skilled jobs." Bantock and others, however, confusingly switch from this particular group, to the "less able," to the "working class," to the "folk," and end up talking about the working class as a whole. Thus, Bantock quotes approvingly from D.H. Lawrence: "The colliers were deeply alive instinctively. But...they avoided, really, the rational aspect of life. They preferred to take life instinctively and intuitively." The facts of working-class history, especially in its political and trades union aspects, surely give the lie to this assertion that the working-class is irrational, but Bantock is performing the same conjuring trick that many so-called radical theorists often turn to by implicitly defining the working-class to suit his own purposes. If you are rational, think ahead, are not the victim of your impulses, then, apparently, you cannot be working-class.

In Bantock's view, working-class culture is defined by the central place given to emotion, instinct, spoken language and immediate, concrete, personal concerns, whereas middle-class culture (and the schools) value reason, thought, the written word and abstract, universal meanings. Thus, the conservative Bantock finds common ground with the radical theorists who see the school as culturally alien to working-class students. The school embodies "a whole set of cultural expectations and requirements that make it not surprising that it is the middle classes that benefit most easily from it. The working-class ethos...contains elements of emotional warmth and a stress on the immediacies of social contact which belie the isolation and intellectualization of the school curriculum. The social conditions of the working class do not encourage the detachment from immediate contacts which the nature of school subjects imposes." On these dubious foundations Bantock proposes for working-class students a curriculum that plays down the cognitive (which they cannot handle) in favour of the affective and artistic, and that devotes three-fifths of its time to dance, movement, music, mime and drama, the media and physical activity. The remaining two-fifths will be concerned with "domestic life," consisting of "home management, preparation for marriage..., some knowledge of human relationships and sex education," with some attention also being given to "the technical, which would exploit especially the boys' interest in some of the mechanical inventions by which they are surrounded."

Despite all this, Bantock insists that "this not an education for helots, an inferior sop handed out to the inadequate..." Not only is it appropriate for many students, and thus not likely to do them psychological damage, but it "provides an entry into many of the greatest riches of our civilization." Nonetheless, it is difficult to avoid the conclusion that it would become a very inferior education. It is based on a profound misreading of working-class history and an apparent lack of any personal experience of working-class culture. It sidesteps consideration of who constitutes the working class, identifying it far too readily with the "less able." It greatly exaggerates the affinity of the middle class for "high culture" while, at the same time, taking far too narrow a view of the virtues of high culture. And it certainly exaggerates the intellectual-cognitive character of the curriculum. Erected on such shaky foundations, this theory of the nature of working-class curriculum is both objectionable and dangerous. Ironically, some of its assumptions are not so different—albeit charged with a different political and philosophical message—from those of some radical "relativist" theorists, which perhaps serves to show some of the ambiguities and difficulties that the concept of a working-class curriculum has to tackle, and how easy it might be for a curriculum that was intended to emancipate and empower working-class students to domesticate and control them.

The Common Curriculum

This is, indeed, the argument of those who argue for a common curriculum, whether on the basis of a liberal-conservative political philosophy, such as Robert Hutchins or Hilda Neatby, from a social-democratic stance, such as Dennis Lawton, or from a Marxist position, such as Brian Simon. This argument rejects the relativism of those who argue that no knowledge is more valuable than any other, and insists instead that the accumulation of human knowledge over the course of history represents an important tradition of which no one should be ignorant and which is itself an important source of enlightenment and empowerment. In many ways, this is the familiar argument for the value of a liberal education, which aims at leading people, in Isaiah Berlin's words, "to find out what kind of world they live in, what they have made, are making, and could make of it…"(Yudkin, 1971, p.10) In this view, knowledge is crucial, for one cannot learn to think seriously about the world without possessing a wide and organized stock of knowledge and the skills to draw upon it. Knowledge as such is neither useless nor class-bound: it is an important element of being human and provides a rich resource upon which to draw in order to see through attempts at manipulation and control and to provide a set of standards against which to assess contemporary society while also providing a sense of alternatives to what exists. It is a view which, while acknowledging the constraints of social class, emphasizes the dignity and freedom of the human being.

This can be explicitly linked to the concept of working-class curriculum, if one insists upon the fundamental importance of the key concepts of demystification and empowerment as aims of education, for neither is attainable in the absence of knowledge. A similar, though not identical, debate took place in the Soviet Union in the early 1920's. At that time those who advocated the creation of a new proletarian culture insisted that this necessitated rejection of all that had gone before, since it was ideologically contaminated and neither of use nor of value in the context of a new society. Proletarian culture, in this view, had no need of bourgeois knowledge, no base in tradition, and no contact with what had been the dominant ideology. It had to make a radical break with the past and begin anew. Such views prompted Lenin himself to intervene in the debate:

> ...only a precise knowledge and transformation of the culture created by the entire development of mankind will enable us to create a proletarian culture. The latter is not clutched out of thin air; it is not an invention of those who call themselves experts in proletarian nature. Proletarian culture must be the logical development of the store of knowledge mankind has accumulated under the yoke of capitalist, landowner, and bureaucratic society. (Lenin, 1966, pp. 467-83)

Nothing is proved, of course, by quoting Lenin, or indeed anyone else, but it is useful to draw attention to the historical dimension of the debate, which is so often overlooked, and to point to the fact that the concept of a working-class curriculum is not inherently "radical," especially when it so easily becomes a form of curricular apartheid in which working-class students are excluded from their wider heritage.

But the question remains as to what portion of that heritage should be taught, since there is obviously far too much of it to include in any single curriculum and since it is dangerously easy to include so much that none of it can be properly assimilated and learning degenerates into a blur of names, dates and facts. Lawton's solution was to turn to Paul Hirst's "forms of knowledge", classifications of knowledge which, Hirst argues, include all its important features and which will serve to introduce students to their human heritage. These forms of knowledge are not subjects, but ways of organizing and conceiving of subjects, and should, according to Hirst, Lawton and others, form the basis of any approach to a coherent, integrated curriculum. In brief they are:

1. formal logic and mathematics;
2. the physical sciences;
3. an awareness and understanding of our own and others' minds;
4. moral judgement and awareness;
5. aesthetic experience;
6. religion;
7. philosophical understanding. (Hirst, 1974)

A Democratic Socialist Approach

Here, then, are the two alternatives: either to design a specifically working-class curriculum or to introduce working-class students to the existing curriculum, with whatever changes might need to be made in it. The first believes that the curriculum should emerge directly from the experience and environment of students; the second prefers a more traditionally academic curriculum but insists that it must incorporate within itself the experience and concerns of students.

Those who support the first alternative reject the second on the grounds that it is simply a form of cultural and ideological domination that dooms too many students to inevitable failure, while rendering them politically harmless. In addition, they argue that when the idea of liberal education for all has been taken seriously, it has never worked. Those who advocate the second alternative argue that we have never really tried it, that we have too easily accepted the apparently common-sense notion that some students are brighter, or more motivated, or harder working than others, and therefore rushed to adjust the curriculum to what appeared to be the facts of student ability. In doing so, however, we have denied far too many students, often though not wholly from the working class, any opportunity to assimilate and exploit the heritage of human knowledge, and we have jumped to the conclusion that this is the result of students' inadequacies, not of the failures of their teachers.

The truth seems to lie in a combination of both views. We must introduce students to important areas of human knowledge while also addressing more immediate concerns. Community education, for example, is not inherently incompatible with liberal education. And liberal education is not a rigid, unchanging entity that students must somehow be seduced or compelled into learning. A recurrent theme in this book has been the importance of connecting the curriculum with issues in the real world and with students' experience. The danger of a specifically working-class curriculum is that it might restrict itself to the students' world, rather than seeking to go beyond it in order to explain it, to show alternatives to it, and to explore ways to change it. Connell, for example, has suggested that any answer to the question of what working-class students should know must go beyond the two alternatives described above, and include them both in a third approach:

> It proposes that working-class kids get access to formal knowledge *via* learning which begins with their own experience and the circumstances which shape it but does not stop there... It draws on existing school knowledge and on what working-class people know already, and organizes this selection of information around problems such as economic survival and collective action, handling the disruption of households, unemployment, responding to the impact of new technology, managing problems of personal identity and association, understanding how schools work and why. (Connell, 1982, pp. 199-200)

There is nothing to object to in any of this and yet it is strangely incomplete. It continues the error of restricting working-class knowledge to problems of immediate and personal concern. But we must, while never ignoring these, always seek to go beyond them. Working-class students, too, have a good deal to learn from history, from literature, from the arts—all of which are as much part of their heritage as they are of anyone else's. One can grasp the limitations of Connell's proposal by extending it to middle-class students and suggesting that they, perhaps, reflect on what they already know, and study such things as foreign travel, investment, divorce, real-estate and the other accoutrements of middle-class life-style. Such a proposal would, presumably, be seen for the absurdity that it is, and certainly would be scorned by most middle-class parents, who want a "proper" education for their children. It is, by this token, difficult to see why working-class children should not get a proper education also.

It is wrong to see them in almost pathological terms and look for special treatments for them, when what they should be receiving, in whatever form is most appropriate, is an education that will accomplish at least these goals. First, education should help them to understand their world in a truly critical sense, not so that they can manipulate or exploit it, and not so that they can simply adapt to it more effectively, but so they can see it as it is, while at the same time, acquiring a sense of alternatives so that they can see it as it might be. Second, education should help students become active participants in the process of gaining control over their own lives, in the triple sense of learning the knowledge and skills necessary for economic survival and independence, for learning to think for themselves, and for participation in the wider social-political process. Third, education should empower students to use their knowledge and skills in the struggle for social change. Fourth, education should give students a sense of community and social solidarity so that they learn to work co-operatively with others and see the social context of their actions. Fifth, education should help students live rich, many-sided lives, so that they can genuinely choose how they want to live. All five principles imply that students should learn not only about their own communities and the issues that face them, and the world in which they live, but also about the wider heritage of which they are both the heirs and the trustees for the generations to come. Any attempt to design a specifically working-class (or indeed any other) curriculum is to be rejected.

It should be emphasized that such a curriculum is intended for all students. It can vary in its details and pedagogy, and even in its content, for the human heritage is vast enough to allow a wide range of selection, but we must reject any attempt to divide the curriculum into university-entrance, commercial, general and other such courses. We must reject also the apparently common-sense notion that only some students have the ability or the aptitude to study an "academic" curriculum. In fact, we would do well to drop the word "academic" altogether, for the kind of curriculum referred to here is intended to be not some theoretical, purely intellectual exercise, but an education for active citizenship that is both theoretical and practical at the same time. One can think of human society as characterized by a continuing debate over the kind of social existence that is most desirable and worthwhile. The debate has been shaped largely by philosophers, writers, politicians and the intellectual elite generally, with occasional interventions by the people at large: education should equip everyone to take note of what is being said and to make their own contribution to it. At the moment we are preparing a minority of students for this, while excluding the majority from any participation, preparing them instead for subordination and non-involvement. This will always be the case while we retain separate programmes for the academic minority and the allegedly non-academic majority, which, inevitably in our current society, broadly divide students along class lines and give them not only a separate curriculum but also a separate pedagogy.

A common curriculum is not a lock-step curriculum. The principles of combining a study of the "real world" with the traditions of liberal education can be shaped into an endless variety of forms, and teachers must have the freedom and the flexibility to adapt and experiment until they find something that interests their students and that is at the same time educationally valuable. Don Sawyer's account of his Newfoundland experience provides a revealing episode when he describes trying to teach ancient civilization to a grade eight class: "My efforts were met with a collective yawn." Then, in a lesson on ancient Israel, a student asked a question about the contemporary Middle East, which proved to be largely unknown to the students: "We had been spending a month and a half on the political shifts of ancient Mesopotamia while one of the major trouble spots of the world was a total mystery." Accordingly, Sawyer, with the help of radio newscasts, turned his attention to the contemporary scene. "This was the start of a process," he comments, "that turned our history class into a study of the social realities of the world, the country and perhaps most significantly, the school, and how these realities affected our lives." (Sawyer, 1979, pp. 62-63)

The Question of Pedagogy

There are, then, many ways to organize and teach such a curriculum, and it is highly probable that no one way will work for all students. We must allow for flexibility and adaptation, especially in those classrooms where it is obvious that students are getting nothing from their experience. When doctors find that one treatment does not work, or produces undesirable side-effects, they search around for something better. In teaching, we all too often seem to conclude that the fault does not lie in the treatment, and even less in the doctor, but only in the patient,who must be forced to take more of the same medicine, and so we go on pumping the same old material down the same unwilling throats, destroying anything of educational value in the process. Connell gets at this when he notes that "the attempt to get most

49

kids to swallow academic knowledge produces insurmountable problems of motivation and control, not only because of the abstractness of the content, but also as a consequence of the formal authority relations of its teaching."(Connell, 1982, p. 199)

There is a point here, but in general it is too bleak a view. If we can change our concept of what it means to be "academic," if we deal with the problems of abstractness and, above all, if we change the authority relations of the teaching—and all these things can be done—many of the problems become solvable. As to how this might be done, one short example must suffice. The task is to teach thirteen-year-olds about the ancient Greek city state, a topic that is suitably abstract and academic, especially for students of that age. The problem is: how to do it? One way is to begin asking about hermits. Do the students know what a hermit is? Whether they do or not, they can be told about some of history's most spectacular examples, such as St. Simeon Stylites living on the top of his tall pillar for most of his life (how did he go to the bathroom?, the students often ask). They can then be asked whether they would like to be hermits and why most people apparently prefer to live together in communities. And how many kinds of communities can they think of? Villages, towns, cities, countries, clans, tribes and the rest usually appear and the simple request for information can turn into an interesting discussion of what comprises a community anyway: is a family a community? A school? An apartment block? And so on and so on. On the basis of all this discussion, the Greek city-state can be presented as yet another form of community. It can be compared with the modern nation-state. Why would Plato or Aristotle deny that a modern city was a community? Would they be right? And so the lesson proceeds. It is, perhaps, academic, but it is certainly not abstract—and radical theorists have too easily assumed that the abstract is by definition inaccessible to students, without looking for ways to make it concrete. And the authority relations of the teaching do not impose an obstacle to students: the teacher retains a privileged position as someone who controls the overall shape of the lesson, who introduces new information at appropriate times, who guides the discussion; at the same time the teacher assigns a major role to students, asking them to draw upon, share and extend what they already know. They are being encouraged to speculate, to guess intelligently, to use their imagination, to pursue open-ended questions. And throughout the lesson, the abstract, academic topic of the Greek city state is being linked to contemporary concerns, focusing on the nature of communities and alternative ways of organizing them.

To repeat an earlier point, this is the kind of pedagogy that is crucial if we are to bridge the gap that exists between the kind of curriculum we would like to teach and the students who are required to take it. It also meets the objection of Bourdieu, Ozolins and others, that a common curriculum is inevitably unequal and unfair because not all students will bring the same personal resources to bear on it. In this view, "...the curriculum of the school cannot be treated as a neutral object: some elements, particularly the letters, humanities and social sciences, are peculiarly dependent on the child's cultural capital. They are taught by a pedagogy which makes continual *implicit* demands on a child's own social and cultural skills of subtlety, nuance, taste and manner which some children acquire naturally from their own cultural milieu *and which are not capable of an explicit pedagogy* ."(Whitty, 1985, p.67) It is worth noting that this is not so much an argument as a series of unsupported assertions. Whether some children are privileged by the curriculum and whether pedagogy can make a difference are questions that have to be investigated. In our present state of knowledge, it makes as much sense to assume that pedagogy can, in fact, achieve a good deal as to assume that it is powerless. And the Bourdieu/Ozolins argument not only grossly inflates the advantages of the middle-class child, at least in Canada, but it takes far too restrictive a view of the capabilities of working-class children, who are perfectly capable of "subtlety, nuance, taste and manner," although it is true that they may not know the correct way to hold a tea-cup and their parents may prefer beer to wine. We should not too quickly assume that working-class students cannot handle the abstract or the allegedly academic.

It should be stressed also that to insist that the traditions of a liberal education must not be excluded from the curriculum is not to take the narrow and snobbish view of high culture that some of its defenders espouse. We are not interested in persuading students that Von Beethoven is better than Van Halen or that the Montreal Symphony Orchestra is superior to the Rolling Stones. Rather, we are interested in looking at music, in all its forms, as a vital form of expression and, in this regard, no form of music is to be excluded or despised. The goal is to stretch students' horizons, to introduce them to aspects of human experience they might not otherwise encounter and to get them to think in new ways about what they already know. What applies to music applies

51

with equal force to art, literature, history and every other subject.

The task is to connect the curriculum with the world of students, but in the context of what Hannan nicely calls a democratic rather than a working-class curriculum: "We do need a good analysis of our heritage of working-class culture. We do also need to keep in mind that we're not merely trying to implant a different class culture. But I don't like thinking of the present division as a choice of alternatives. A democratic curriculum will be a synthesis of these conflicting class cultures. Thus, we do not expect our kids to throw away their working-class, or ethnic, language heritage, but we do not expect them to know only that."(Hannan, 1985, p.255) In short, the issue is not one of choosing between a working-class curriculum and liberal education, but of combining them.

In this process, pedagogy will obviously hold pride of place. Equally or more important is the task of changing the hidden curriculum of schooling. What offends many students at school is their relegation to the role of powerless recipients of other peoples' information. They have little voice in what they will study, or in how they will study it. Some of them grow to accept this, with more or less resignation; others simply reject the whole experience. If we can alter the status of the learner in relationship to what is being learned, we will probably find that education begins to look very different, both for students and for teachers. And while the schools will never in existing circumstances totally escape their role as instruments of social control, they will nonetheless be able to work as vehicles of a genuine education, aimed at empowerment, demystification and enlightenment, dedicated to the pursuit of "really useful knowledge."

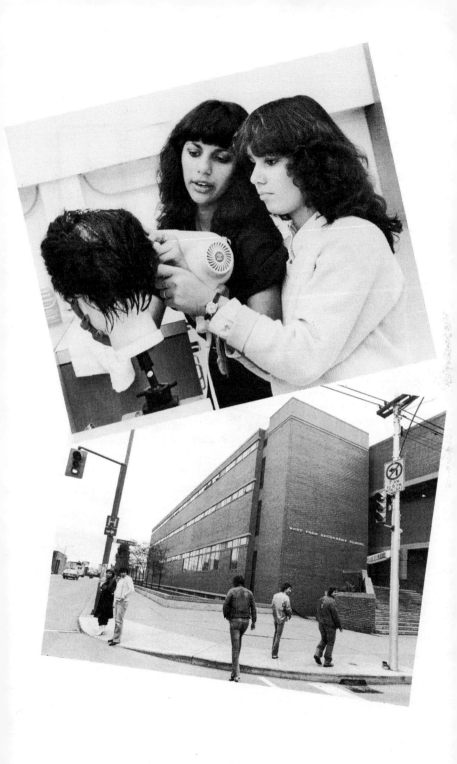

Chapter 4

Nationalism, Citizenship and Curriculum

Democratic Socialism and National Education

Socialists have been historically opposed to the use of education to promote nationalism in the young. With others, they have long argued that the schools should teach international and global awareness and solidarity. Thus it would seem contradictory for Canadian socialists to press for Canadian schools to cultivate Canadian national sentiment, were it not for three important considerations. First, there is a realization that, as things currently stand in Canada, the alternative to Canadian nationalism is not a spirit of internationalism, but domination by the United States. Second, Canadian socialists insist that Canadian society is worth preserving; that, with all its imperfections, it constitutes a basis for the nurturing of socialist values; and that, however gravely it may be threatened, it makes possible a way of life that is different from and preferable to the one found, for example, in the United States. Third, their view of Canadian nationalism is neither aggressive nor exclusive, but quite compatible with internationalism and indeed a necessary step towards it.

More fundamentally, Canadian socialists cannot work in a vacuum. We must begin somewhere and the most obvious and practical place is our own society. It should be self-evident that Canadian students must learn about the society of which they are a part. It is of little use to teach them about utopian fantasies of future global interdependence if it means ignoring the problems of the here and now. The task is, of course, to link the two, so that to-day's utopian fantasies cease to be either fantastic or utopian. For all these reasons, any attempt to see

Canadian education in a socialist framework, and especially one that is centrally concerned with citizenship, must take into account the national question.

In 1968 a bombshell hit Canadian educational circles. At first sight, it looked harmless enough: a slim volume bearing the title *What Culture? What Heritage?* and the subtitle "a study of civic education in Canada." Very quickly, however, the book gained national attention. It proved to be far more than a report on education, since it raised fundamental questions of national identity and even of the possible disappearance of Canada. So far as the strictly educational aspects of the report were concerned, it described itself as presenting "a very strong indictment of the way Canadian studies are now being taught in our schools." More broadly, the report argued that the teaching of Canadian studies in the schools was, with a few exceptions, worse than useless, producing in students a boredom and a cynicism that were a threat to national existence.

What Hodgetts did for the schools in 1968, T.H.B. Symons did for the universities in 1975. Symons investigated the universities thoroughly and reported a startling absence of Canadian content and Canadian materials in the university curriculum. Even more disturbing, "there was a tremendous doubt about whether it was academically appropriate or worthwhile or legitimate or dignified for schools and teachers to pay attention to Canadian questions. Also there was downright hostility or disdain..."(Symons, 1975, p.13)

In all the discussion and activity that followed the publication of these and other documents, a number of questions recurred frequently: just what should be the connection between education, whatever the level, and nationalism? To what extent should education be placed at the service of the nation-state? Who was to define what the national interest was? Should there be a national policy, not to mention a national department of government, for education? In educational terms, what should be the balance between national and regional interests?

With some exceptions, the idea that education should promote and strengthen any one particular conception of national unity was rejected. The very diversity of Canadian society, it was argued, made such concepts divisive. As Hodgetts put it in *What Culture? What Heritage?* : "Programs based on our concept of Canadianism would make it impossible to teach national unity, but they could help our young people to develop an intelligent, knowledgeable affection for their country and a critically responsible interest in it."(Hodgetts, 1968, p.121) Symons agreed: "Patriotic appeals to preserve and develop Canadian identity do not constitute, in practice or in principle, an adequate rationale for Canadian studies at any level of education."(Symons, 1975, p.12) This was partly because the very concepts of unity and identity were themselves contested; they were matters of debate rather than of consensus; and part of the reality of the Canadian experience was and is that they are open-ended questions for continuing discussion rather than truths that have been decided once and for all. It also arose from a conviction that education, at all levels, should be a matter of opening minds, not closing them, of teaching students to think and to deal with issues critically and independently. Thus, the key words were knowledge, understanding, awareness.

The debate that began in the late 1960's continues into the present and, indeed, is the contemporary version of something that is as old as Canada itself. Here, for example, is Vincent Massey in 1926:

> In a country with so scattered a population as ours and a vast frontier exposed to alien influences, the task of creating a truly national feeling must inevitably be arduous, but this is the undertaking to which our education systems must address themselves, for by true education alone will the problems be solved. To our schools we must look for the good Canadian.
> (Milburn, 1972, p. 100)

The key questions are all here: what does it mean to be a "good Canadian?" What is a "truly national feeling?" For that matter, what is "true education?" And how can education cope with the "alien influences" that come from the United States as well as with the regionalism that derives from Canada's history and from its scattered population? In broad terms, what should and can the schools do to maintain and strengthen the existence of Canada as an independent state?

As early as the 1890's there had been attempts to answer these questions by providing a truly national history textbook which would be acceptable to all groups in all regions of the country. Although such a book was produced, it proved to be far from universally acceptable. The fundamental problem lay in the lack of any agreement on how to define the Canadian nation. Then, as now, for most Anglophone Canadians Canada is a nation, or, if it is not, it should be. For many Francophone

Québécois, Canada is a state, a political entity; but it is not a nation, not a cultural unit. In the latter view, Quebec represents a nation, while Canada does not. Given this basic disagreement, fundamental problems arise for any attempt to create a national education policy. Indeed, in the 1980's such a policy has become even more problematic as Canada's native peoples lay claim to the right of nationhood and as multicultural policies are entrenched in much of Canada, thereby reducing even further the possibility of one universally acceptable version of Canadian history.

The question may then be phrased as: How can a national education policy be national in any meaningful sense while at the same time acknowledging the rights of both official language groups, of regionalism, of multiculturalism, of native rights, and the political reality of provincial/territorial control of curricula and programmes?

A useful distinction here is that made by Ramsay Cook between the concepts of the nation-state and the nationalist-state. The former is primarily a legal and political unit in which individual and group rights are respected and protected and in which diversity is not only tolerated but encouraged, with no attempt being made to propagate any one official ideology or culture, except to insist upon the observation of consonant broad principles such as tolerance, respect for human rights and obedience to the law. The latter, the nationalist-state, is one which, by contrast, does propagate an official culture and which sees itself as far more than a legal and political unit, since it is committed to certain fundamental values. In Ramsay Cook's words, "The nationalist-state is one in which the ideological demands of one cultural group or nation are forced upon all other groups within its borders."(Cook, 1987, p.5) If Canada is to survive, and if it is to encourage the diversity that is its very essence, it is the ideal of the nation-state, not the nationalist-state, that must pervade the curriculum. In the words of the Royal Commission on Bilingualism and Biculturalism (1963-69):

> An understanding of contemporary society is inade-
> quate if it is based on narrow exclusiveness. Even if one
> thinks solely in terms of French Canadian or English
> Canadian society, the social purpose of history is best
> achieved by a conscious effort to explain the different
> values and aspirations of the two societies when con-
> troversies arise. But if any textbook lays claim to being
> a history of Canada, it must go much further. It must be

the history of both societies... The establishment and
survival of French Canada is a significant aspect of Canadian history and so is the establishment and survival
of Canada as a political union in North America. Any
Canadian history textbook should present both these
themes. (Milburn, 1972, pp. 173-8)

We must not so much teach students this or that version of the
Canadian reality, and even less should we pretend that there is one
official or objectively correct version, but rather we should introduce
students to the continuing Canadian debate by teaching them about the
various interpretations of what Canada is and should be, and by giving
them the knowledge and the skills to make up their own minds. It is not
so much teaching them to understand *the* Canadian identity as teaching
them what the various interpretations of Canadian identity (or identi-
ties) are.

We must then abandon the practice of using conventional definitions of nationality and nationhood with their emphasis upon uni-
formity and officially approved values. We must learn to see these
definitions not as timeless and objective realities but rather as historical constructions of the European nationalist movements of the nineteenth century with their insistence that each "nation" should have its
own unique geographical boundaries and political state. This nineteenth century nationalist dogma is, in fact, a fundamental interruption
in a much older tradition of multi-ethnic, multi-lingual, multi-racial
political units, of which the Roman Empire is a classic example, with
its willingness to confer citizenship upon all who were willing to
undertake the accompanying obligations, regardless of their ethnic or
racial background. The nineteenth century concept of nationalism,
which continues to exert a powerful influence in our own time, does not
apply to Canada and, when it is so applied, Canada must inevitably be
found defective. Canada, with its French-English duality, its multiculturalism, its diversity, can never be a nation-state in the conventional
sense, and any attempt to make it so will be as destructive as it is
unrealistic.

Paradoxically, Canadian schools will best serve their national
purpose by de-nationalizing students, that is to say, by showing them
that the conventionally accepted notion of the nation-state is a historical, time-bound, ideological construct that should not be allowed to
stand unchallenged and that is neither desirable nor appropriate when

applied to Canada. We must see questions of Canadian identity, of national unity, of what it means to be Canadian, precisely as questions, that can be explored and investigated and that will yield a variety of answers, not as dogmas placed beyond question and accepted undisturbed. To return to Ramsay Cook's distinction, we must show students the difference between the concepts of the nation-state and the nationalist-state and their implications for Canada. This means also abandoning the tradition of using the schools as an instrument for assimilating children into some officially approved version of Canadianism.

What Should Students Know About Canada?

Some years ago Hodgetts and Gallagher worried aloud that the discipline of Canadian studies was galloping off in all directions and argued that "what is needed now... is a common framework of ideas that educators in all provinces should use in the development of Canada studies that will be country-wide in perspectives and objectives." They certainly addressed themselves to the right questions, though their answers are open to challenge. They insisted that the crucial question was (and is): "what should young Canadians understand about their country?" Their answer was that any curriculum or programme that addressed this question must be based on "the analysis of Canada as a political community," with the concept of political community being understood as "simply a convenient, value-free term... to describe any group of people living within recognized, clearly defined geographic boundaries, having a system of government and other shared institutions, and possibly a minimum set of goals." Hodgetts and Gallagher acknowledged that a political community, and especially the Canadian version, contains many groups "based on such factors as family, neighbourhood, region, ethnic origin, religion, language, occupation, and economic status" (the closest they came to mentioning social class) and that "controversy and tension... are inevitable in society." Indeed, it is precisely these controversies and tensions that should lie at the heart of the curriculum and that make Canadian studies so important: "A political community also requires a minimum ability among its citizens to resolve conflict with tolerance, knowledge, and understanding of opposing viewpoints. Without this ability, the tensions may cease to be beneficial and become debilitating or destructive." On this basis, Hodgetts and Gallagher proposed that Canadian studies programmes

should encompass these "four separate but inter-related components":
1.   the Canadian environment;
2.   the structure and functioning of government;
3.   the essential characteristics and functioning of the Canadian economic system;
4.   public issues in Canada.

These four components, in turn, were designed to illustrate the "readily identifiable characteristics or basic features that collectively make Canada a unique country," and were described as follows:
1.   Canada is a northern, vast and regionally divided country.
2.   Canada has a broad natural resource base composed of both renewable and non-renewable resources.
3.   Canada is an industrial, technological and urbanized society.
4.   Canada is a culturally diverse, multi-ethnic country with two historically predominant linguistic and cultural groups.
5.   Canada is exposed to a multitude of external economic, political and cultural influences. (Hodgetts & Gallagher, 1978, *passim*)

Here, then, is an attempt to see Canada whole and to teach students what makes it tick. One can applaud the attempt without accepting it in every detail. Hodgetts and Gallagher were right to insist that careful thought had to be given to the purpose of teaching students about Canada, and to insist that it was not good enough simply to bundle more Canadian subject matter into the curriculum. Their idea of providing some kind of model also has much to commend it, and it should be stressed that they were speaking not of any one course but rather of a framework that would guide curriculum planning from kindergarten to the end of high school.

Fundamentally, the question is this: What should students have learned about Canada by the time they finish high school? How this is done can be decided only at the local level: the choice of grade levels and subjects, the sequencing of subject-matter, the formulating of objectives and all such technical questions cannot be settled in one simple formula. Rather, what is needed is a grid that can be placed over a curriculum in order to see what it includes and what it omits, and to provide some basis for analysis and revision. At the same time, it must be emphasized that no such grid can ever be fully satisfactory: it is itself a basis for discussion, analysis and revision. But discussion has to begin somewhere and the grid can provide a useful starting point, even if it is totally scrapped and replaced by something different. For what is needed is really very simple. Those of us who see the Canadian context of school curricula as important must engage in a continuing debate over what precisely schools should be teaching and work to ensure that it be taught—and learned. Here, then, is such a formulation:

1.　　Canada is a country in which national unity cannot be taken for granted. It is officially bilingual, culturally diverse and subject to often severe centrifugal forces. Many of its various cultural groups are experiencing a new sense of identity.

Students should:
(a)　know the variety of cultural groups that comprise Canada;
(b)　know the major issues between Anglophone and Francophone Canada;
(c)　know the history of English-French relations in Canada;
(d)　be able to compare Canada with other multi-lingual countries (e.g. Switzerland, Belgium);
(e)　know about cultural/ethnic/racial antagonisms in Canada past and present;
(f)　know about the situation of native peoples in Canada;
(g)　know the pros and cons of the various ideals of Canada (e.g. unitary, bi-national, multi-cultural, bilingual).

2.　　Canada is characterized by strong feelings of regionalism, a result of history, geography and economic relationships.

Students should:
(a)　know about the major regions of Canada: their terrain, climate, economy, lifestyle;
(b)　know about the different perceptions of Canada characteristically held in each region;

(c) know how regionalism has affected Canada historically;
(d) assess the varying interpretations and assessments of the role of regionalism in Canada;

3. Canada is exposed to strong external influences, especially from the United States.

Students should:
(a) know why there are such strong external influences;
(b) know the advantages/disadvantages derived by Canada from its proximity to the U.S.A.;
(c) know the current issues and relationships between Canada and the U.S.A.;
(d) evaluate different solutions proposed for Canadian-U.S. tensions;
(e) understand similarities and differences between Canadian and American society.

4. Canada is an industrialized, technological and urbanized society, although to varying degrees in different regions. This creates both benefits and problems.

Students should:
(a) know the geography of Canada and its regions;
(b) know the history of technology, urbanization, labour and industrial development in Canada;
(c) know about regional disparities in Canada and attempts to overcome them;
(d) know the different theories concerning the impact of modern industry, technology, urban growth and population settlement;
(e) assess the pros and cons of various forms of urban and rural life;
(f) assess the various prognoses of and solutions to the problems of urban, technological society.

5. Canada's political system is that of a liberal parliamentary democracy. Canada is federally organized, with consequent federal/provincial tensions.

Students should:

(a)   know how "political systems" operate at different levels (e.g. classroom, school, municipality, etc.);

(b)   know the structure of Canada's political system— with special reference to how it works in *practice* rather than in theory (e.g. the role of pressure groups, decision-making processes, etc.);

(c)   know the federal-provincial government structuring of Canada;

(d)   compare the Canadian political system with others;

(e)   evaluate the different solutions proposed for problems of federal-provincial relations;

(f)   understand the major problems facing Canada.

6.   Canada is undergoing a trend towards larger and larger institutions—both governmental and non-governmental— against which individuals feel that they have little or no power.

Students should:

(a)   identify the larger institutions;

(b)   know that a trend to larger institutions is taking place (e.g. in work-place, government, etc.) and know the reasons for this;

(c)   determine the pros and cons of the phenomenon;

(d)   assess the various solutions/suggestions to overcome its impact.

7.   Canada is experiencing a serious ecological crisis, exemplified by industrial pollution in some parts of the country, and generally, by the dilemma that pits the demand for energy against the demand to preserve natural environments and to respect the rights of particular groups of people.

Students should:

(a)   be familiar with current ecological problems;

(b)   be familiar with the cause of the ecological dilemma (locally, regionally, and globally);

(c)   be familiar with the various points of view (no

growth, limited growth, laissez-faire, etc.);
(d) evaluate the implications of the "ecological di-
      lemma."

8. Canada has one of the highest material standards of living
in the world, although poverty still exists in specific areas or
among specific groups of people.

Students should:
(a) know the extent and impact of poverty in Canada;
(b) compare the Canadian standard of living with others
      around the world;
(c) examine some of the possible causes of poverty;
(d) know and evaluate efforts to alleviate/abolish pov-
      erty, both governmental and non-governmental.

9. Canada has a mixed economy with inequities in the distribution of wealth and power. This produces considerable debate
and disagreement on the role of the state vis-à-vis the role of
private business.

Students should:
(a) know basically how economic systems work;
(b) know the main features of the Canadian economic
      system;
(c) be familiar with the distribution of wealth and power
      in Canada, and its intersection with social class;
(d) examine the dominant forms of economic systems in
      the world (planned/market/mixed);
(e) examine current economic problems in Canada;
(f) evaluate proposals for economic change in Canada.

10. Canada is an economically developed middle-power with
various aims and responsibilities.

Students should:
(a) know the nature of Canada's world position;
(b) know the historical background of Canada's world
      position;

(c) know what involvement Canada has with international trade and investment;

(d) know Canada's relationships with the Third World;

(e) assess the position of Canada in world affairs and the possible directions Canada should take in the future.

11. Canada is a society based upon a commitment to human and constitutional rights.

Students should:

(a) know the main elements of the Constitution and the Charter of Rights and Freedoms;

(b) assess the strengths and weaknesses of the existing formulation of human rights, and of alternative formulations;

(c) know how human rights are protected;

(d) know the violations of human rights past and present;

(e) be familiar with current issues of racism and sexism;

(f) be personally committed to human rights.

12. Canada has a rich artistic and cultural tradition.

Students should:

(a) know the main elements of the history of the arts in Canada;

(b) understand the role of the arts in society;

(c) understand the issues facing the arts in Canada today;

(d) acquire an adequate knowledge of and an interest in/ taste for the arts.

13. Canada is a society characterized by low rates of political/ social involvement.

Students should:

(a) know the data concerning political participation in Canada;

(b) understand the relationship between participation, power and class;

(c) acquire the skills and dispositions necessary for participation.

14. Canada is a society that frequently debates what kind of society it should be.

Students should:
(a) know the main elements of this debate, e.g. concerning the role of regionalism, federalism, language, the nature of government;
(b) assess the various proposals put forward from time to time concerning the future of Canada;
(c) form a personal assessment of the kind of society Canada should be;
(d) assess the various philosophies of society, e.g. conservatism, liberalism, socialism, anarchism, etc.

It bears repeating that these fourteen statements are not intended to form the basis of a course of study, but rather to describe what students should be learning about Canada during their twelve or so years of public schooling and from whatever combination of subjects. Nothing is said here about how this might best be accomplished, for such decisions can only be made in light of local circumstances. The list is intended to be neither exhaustive nor definitive. It is offered simply as a starting-point for discussion and as a way to give concrete form to an otherwise abstract issue. It deals mainly with content; it describes what students should know. As it stands, it could obviously be arid and boring, though every attempt has been made to link what is to be known with the world in which students find themselves. Nonetheless, if it is to come to life in the classroom, much will obviously depend upon how it is taught. It should also be emphasized that more than arm-chair, theoretical knowledge is intended. We will not have accomplished very much if students only learn what is suggested here in order to pass a test or get a mark. What the philosopher A.N. Whitehead once called "inert ideas" are not enough. The reason for teaching students about Canada, after all, is to enable them to take part in the continuing debate about what kind of society Canada is and should be, to give them the tools to take more control of their own lives and of the direction of Canadian society. As described elsewhere, knowledge must be linked to commitment and action, in a framework of respect for democratic values.

Canadian Studies and World Studies

In devoting so much attention to Canada, we should not forget that it is important to devote adequate time and attention to the rest of the world. There is a danger that in our concern to make sure that students learn about their own country, we might forget how important it is for them to learn about others. In an age when international problems are of obviously increasing importance, and when they inevitably impinge upon Canadians' lives, it seems self-defeating to ignore the rest of the world, or to leave students to discover it through the vagaries of chance and television—which usually means they see it through U.S. eyes. As things now stand, however, most students leave high school with little more than the most basic knowledge of, say, the Soviet Union, communism, Africa, the Middle East, the arms race, problems of development and so on. And, even then, their knowledge is often drawn, directly or indirectly, from U.S. sources, so that they see the world through American rather than Canadian (and never through French, or Soviet, or Chinese, or Algerian) eyes.

There are useful courses in world affairs in most high school curricula (though it is not at all certain that taking one course will accomplish the kind of global literacy that is needed in the modern world) but they are elective courses, taken by only a minority of students. Perhaps one of the worst features of the Americanization of Canadian children's view of the world is its failure to treat the world seriously on its own terms, but to see it only as a vehicle for American policy interests. Canadian students by and large know little or nothing even of Canada's role in the Cold War, in the United Nations, in Southern Africa, in disarmament negotiations, let alone of the history and current status of China, the Soviet Union and other major countries. In their understandable concern to ensure that Canada was dealt with adequately in the curriculum, Canadian nationalists failed to ask themselves what was the best balance between national and global concerns. The challenge now facing Canadian studies in the schools is to find a way of combining these two emphases that will do justice to both.

This is more than simply a question of establishing a proper balance between the attention given in the curriculum to Canadian and non-Canadian topics. The reality is that we now live in a world fundamentally different from that of a generation or so ago and students must be properly equipped for living in it, both for its sake and for theirs, for, as has been often pointed out, we continue to live by old assumptions and conceptions which can be positively dangerous in the changed circumstances of today. Einstein said it best when he observed in 1946 that "the unleashed power of the atom has changed everything save our modes of thinking, and thus we drift toward unparalleled catastrophe." Einstein was speaking specifically of atomic power and nuclear weapons but his words can be applied equally to the issues of environmental exploitation, of international economic development, of north-south relations and of social justice, all of which might prove to be as dangerous and disastrous as nuclear war itself. The world is no longer a collection of autonomous states that can all act independently, doing whatever they think is best for their own interests, without concerning themselves unduly with the consequences for others. The world has become an interlocking system in which, as in any system, movement in one part sets up reaction in others, often in unforeseen and unpredictable ways. The old liberal assumption that the greatest good of the greatest number can be achieved by everyone acting in their own particular interests was always shaky: in today's world it is a recipe for disaster. In a superficial way we have accepted this new reality as we have become familiar with new ways of describing the world: global village, spaceship earth, north-south dialogue, interdependence—such phrases have almost become clichés devoid of the power to make us think.

Increasingly, the major problems that face the world can be solved only by international action. This is certainly true of such problems as economic development, refugees, population growth, distribution of goods and resources, environmental damage and, above all, disarmament. For the first time, the planet itself is in danger.

Running through all these issues is a question not so much of survival or prudence, but of simple justice. Can we live comfortably and with easy consciences in a world where so many people live so miserably? Even more, can we face the fact that our prosperity is itself partly based on the poverty and exploitation of other parts of the world? Are we prepared to consider that foreign aid in its present forms is often exploitation in polite disguise? These are not at all abstract, far-away problems beyond the scope of the ordinary person. We live in an age where even eating a hamburger may have entailed raising beef on land torn from rainforest whose depletion is likely to have serious climatic and environmental consequences. In such a context, the phrase "think globally, act locally," has profound consequences for personal living and education.

What then should students learn about the world in their schools, whether through a distinct course of study or as a body of knowledge distributed across the curriculum and throughout their school lives? As with the preceding list of Canadian topics, it should be remembered that what follows is intended as a basis for discussion rather than as a definitive programme. It is offered as a framework either for designing a new programme or for examining an existing programme, and it is intended to describe what students should have learnt not in any given year but as the cumulative result of all their schoolwork. It should be noted also that this list describes only *what* students should know. It says nothing about the skills and values that should accompany this knowledge, and without which it is nothing more than armchair theory, as is explained in the following section of this chapter. The knowledge that students acquire in school should familiarize them with the main features that characterize the world in which they will spend their lives and with the issues to which they give rise. They are as follows:

1. The great and increasing disparity between the developed and the developing countries.

Students should:
(a) know the main differences between the developed and developing worlds and explore the meanings of the concept of "development";
(b) know the connections that exist between the developed and developing worlds (e.g. through aid, development programmes, trade, tourism, and so on;
(c) examine the political and other problems that exist between the developed and developing worlds;
(d) evaluate the different diagnoses of the problems and the different proposed solutions to these problems;
(e) formulate a personal position on the whole issue of development.

2. The impact of science and technology.

Students should:
(a) be familiar with scientific methods, principles and knowledge;
(b) know the ways in which science and technology have an impact on modern society;
(c) compare this impact with that of other features of modern society;
(d) evaluate the different positions advanced concerning the impact of science and technological development (i.e. the "curse or blessing" arguments).

3. The threat of war, especially in view of the existence of nuclear weapons, great power strategies and international alliance systems.

Students should:
(a) know the effects and risks of nuclear war, and about the various theories and policies advocated to prevent it (i.e. from pacifism to deterrence);
(b) be familiar with the history of the arms race and super-power strategies and policies;
(c) know something about current crises, e.g. Central America, Middle East, Southern Africa.

4. The urgency of the ecological question and the growing pressure on resources.

Students should:
(a) know the main principles of ecology;
(b) evaluate the different positions advanced concerning the present danger (or lack of danger) to the environment;
(c) analyze, via particular examples, the dilemma of the need for resources versus the need to preserve ecological balance on both the global and local levels.

5. The lack of basic human rights in many parts of the world, especially where racist regimes are in power.

Students should:
(a) decide what are human rights;
(b) evaluate the different conceptions of human rights and how to protect them;
(c) examine what is like to live under a regime that denies human rights;
(d) know about different regimes, past and present, and their policies on human rights.

6. The importance of ideology as a way of organizing a world-view and of organizing society.

Students should:
(a) know the salient features of the major ideologies that have affected twentieth century life (e.g. anarchism, fascism, marxism, liberal-democracy, capitalism, socialism);
(b) analyze and evaluate these ideologies;
(c) know about the role that ideologies play in human affairs, especially as reflected in the history of the twentieth century.

7. The growing trend towards larger and larger institutions against which the individual feels increasingly powerless (e.g. big government, the trans-national corporation).

Students should:
(a) know about the historical development of large institutions (e.g. the growth of government, of labour unions, of corporations, of communities) and the reasons for this;
(b) evaluate the pros and cons of this development;
(c) understand the phenomenon of alienation, evaluate its validity and assess its origins.

8. The revolution of rising expectations, by which most people wish, and indeed expect, their living conditions to improve steadily.

Students should:
(a) compare the way of life today with that in other historical eras;
(b) know about the phenomenon of rising expectations and the unforeseen problems it has produced;
(c) evaluate the ways in which people are attempting to deal with these problems;
(d) examine the relationship between quality of life and material prosperity.

9. The interconnectedness of the world.

Students should:
(a) know how the different regions and people of the world are interconnected (trade, investment, alliances, etc.);
(b) know how these interconnections affect the world;
(c) know and assess the impact of such phenomena as modern communications, international trade patterns, increasing contact between governments and people, trans-national corporations;
(d) know the work of key international organizations, especially the United Nations.

10. The demographic phenomena of the "population explosion" and of large-scale movements of people.

Students should:
(a) know about the population explosion, its causes and its effects;
(b) evaluate the different positions advanced concerning population growth;
(c) evaluate the different policies in force around the world that are attempting to deal with demographic problems.

11. The rapidity and pervasiveness of change, so that the ten previous items may well become obsolete.

Students should:

(a) know how change has occurred in different eras;
(b) know how change is occurring today;
(c) evaluate the different arguments advanced concerning the impact of contemporary social change;
(d) examine possible future trends in the world;
(e) give some thought to the kind of world they would prefer to see come into existence.

Active Citizenship and Democratic Socialist Education

To describe those aspects of Canada and the world with which students should have some familiarity is necessarily to talk in terms of knowledge, but it cannot be repeated too often that knowledge alone is not enough unless it is linked with commitment and action. To adapt a well-known maxim: it is one thing to understand the world, but the important task is to change it. To repeat an earlier argument, the task of education, from a democratic socialist perspective, is:

1. to help students to see the world as it is;
2. to help them see it as it might be; and
3. to give them the skills and dispositions to transform one into the other.

This involves a shift in values and assumptions and a rethinking of long-accepted and conventional ways of thinking and acting. This has best been described by the physicist Frijthof Capra and those socialists who have taken to heart the arguments of feminism and contemporary environmentalists. Briefly put, it means leading students to rethink their assumptions in the following ways:

From	*To*
A view of the universe as a collection of separate pieces that can be dealt with in isolation or in a linear way.	An integrated view of the universe as a system in which everything is connected.

From	*To*
An individualistic view that sees self-interest as the guiding principle in life and sees individuals as separate one from another.	An emphasis upon connections and interdependence.
An emphasis upon competition.	An emphasis upon co-operation.
An emphasis upon expansion and growth; taking resources and the environment for granted.	An emphasis upon conservation, and the wise use of resources.
An emphasis upon control, domination, exploitation.	An emphasis upon integration, stewardship.
A preoccupation with the here and now and the short-term.	A concern for the future and the long-term.

As Capra himself summed it up, this new way of looking at and acting in the world "recognizes the unjust and destructive dynamics of patriarchy; it calls for social responsibility and a sound sustainable economic system; it rejects all forms of exploitation, of nature as well as of people; and it includes a commitment to non-violence at all levels."(Capra, 1982, *passim*)

There is much that schools can do to facilitate this transformation, both formally and informally. Above all, we can operate our classrooms in this spirit so that we teach as much by example as by any direct message. In Toronto, for example, the Parents for Peace group has emphasized the importance of the "peaceful classroom," one that helps children "to decrease competition and increase cooperation, to still aggression and promote helpfulness to divert ostracism and encourage acceptance." Such classrooms are based upon three foundations:

73

1. students must have a sense that the classroom is theirs;
2. there must be problem-solving approaches in which the teachers and students work together;
3. there must be mutual respect among the students and between them and their teachers.

The Parents for Peace also suggest six criteria for organizing school-work in order to promote appropriate values:

1. work must allow for student choice;
2. self-expression must be encouraged;
3. cooperative activities must be stressed;
4. activities that promote a sense of self-worth must be emphasized;
5. students must engage in the exploration of social values;
6. learning must connect with the real world through current events, at local and world levels.

Teaching methods also should reflect and promote the outlooks and values that the new way of looking at the world entails. In this connection, the Club of Rome makes an important distinction between what it calls "maintenance learning" and "innovative learning." The former is what we do now and consists of "fixed outlooks, methods and rules for dealing with known and recurring situations."(Botkin, 1979, p.43) To use a more familiar term, it is education as problem-solving. It assumes, however, that the problems are identifiable or at least unlikely to differ much from those that have arisen in the past, and that traditional methods will be adequate. While necessary, such a learning style is inadequate in today's world and must be accompanied by an emphasis upon innovative learning, which stresses not the learning of known skills for dealing with known problems, but the ability to anticipate the unknown. In the words of the Club of Rome it is "a necessary means of preparing individuals and societies to act in concert in new situations." In summary form, it involves the following changes:

Maintenance Learning	*Innovative Learning*
Problem-solving	Problem-formulating
Value-conserving	Value-creating

Adaptation *Maintenance Learning*	Anticipation *Innovative Learning*
Following leaders	Participation
Emphasis on the Past	Focus on the Future
Conformity	Autonomy
Learning facts	Critical judgment
Analysis	Integration
Emphasis on the national	Global orientation

It should be emphasized that what is suggested here is not a diametrically opposed shift of direction from one of the above modes of learning to the other but rather a blending of the two, with a reduced emphasis upon the former, which still receives pride of place in most classrooms. How this might reflect itself in actual lessons and teaching techniques is illustrated elsewhere; whatever is done, the fundamental point is that, in examining what students learn, we should not ignore how they are learned and are taught. Active, participating citizenship depends upon active, participating schools and both must become part of the democratic socialist agenda.

BIBLIOGRAPHY

Alberta Department of Education, *Programme of Studies for Senior High Schools*. Edmonton, 1978.

M. Apple, *Education and Power*. London: Routledge & Kegan Paul, 1982.

M. Apple, *Ideology and Curriculum*. London: Routledge & Kegan Paul, 1979.

R.W. Bibby & D.C. Posterski, *The Emerging Generation: An Inside Look at Canada's Teenagers*. Toronto: Irwin, 1985.

J.W. Botkin et al., *No Limits to Learning: Bridging the Human Gap*. Oxford: Pergamon, 1979.

P. Bourdieu & J.C. Passeron, *Reproduction in Education, Society and Culture*. London: Sage, 1977.

W. Boyd, *The Educational Theory of Jean-Jacques Rousseau*. London: Macmillan, 1912.

F. Capra, *The Turning-Point: Science, Society and the Rising Culture*. New York: Simon & Schuster, 1982.

A. Chaiton & N. McDonald (eds.), *Canadian Schools and Canadian Identity*. Toronto: Gage, 1977.

J. Clarke et al., *Working Class Culture: Studies in History and Theory*. London: Hutchinson/Centre for Contemporary Cultural Studies, 1979.

R. Connell et al., *Making the Difference: Schools, Families and Social Division*. Sydney: Allen & Unwin, 1982.

R. Cook, *The Maple Leaf Forever: Essays on Nationalism and Politics in Canada*. 1977.

W. Cowburn, *Class, Ideology and Community Education*. London: Croom Helm, 1986.

H. Entwhistle, *Antonio Gramsci: Conservative Schooling for Radical Politics*. London: Routledge & Kegan Paul, 1979.

H. Entwhistle, *Class, Culture and Education*. London: Methuen, 1978.

M. French, *Beyond Power: On Women, Men and Morals*. New York: Summit, 1985.

H. Giroux, *Theory and Resistance in Education*. Massachusetts: Bergin & Garvey, 1983.

J. Goodlad, *A Place Called School*. New York: McGraw Hill, 1984.

W. Hannan, *Democratic Curriculum*. Sydney: Allen & Unwin, 1985.

D.H. Hargreaves, *The Challenge for the Comprehensive School:*

Culture, Curriculum and Community. London: Routledge & Kegan Paul, 1982.

K. Harris, *Teachers and Classes: A Marxist Analysis*. London: Routledge & Kegan Paul, 1982.

P.H. Hirst, *Knowledge and the Curriculum*. London: Routledge & Kegan Paul, 1974.

A.B. Hodgetts, *What Culture? What Heritage?* Toronto: O.I.S.E., 1968.

A.B. Hodgetts & P. Gallagher, *Teaching Canada for the '80s*. Toronto: O.I.S.E., 1978.

R.Hoggart, *The Uses of Literacy*. London: Chatto & Windus, 1957.

J. Hohl, *Les enfants n' aiment pas la pédagogie*. Montreal: Editions St. Martin, 1982.

S. Humphries, *Hooligans or Rebels: An Oral History of Working Class Childhood and Youth 1889-1939*. Oxford: Blackwell, 1981.

K. Jones, *Beyond Progressive Education*. London: Macmillan, 1983.

D.S. Landes, *The Unbound Prometheus: Technological Change and Industrial Development in Europe from 1750 to the Present*. Cambridge: Cambridge University Press, 1969.

D. Lawton, *Class, Culture and the Curriculum*. London: Routledge & Kegan Paul, 1975.

V.I. Lenin, *Selected Works*, Vol. 9. London: Lawrence & Wishart.

D.W. Livingstone et al., *Critical Pedagogy and Cultural Power*. Toronto: Garamond, 1987.

S. Lukes, *Emile Durkheim: His Life and Work*. New York: Harper & Row, 1972.

A. Lunacharsky, *On Education: Selected Articles and Speeches*. Moscow: Progress, 1981.

C.B. Macpherson, *The Life and Times of Liberal Democracy*. Oxford: Oxford University Press, 1977.

Manitoba Department of Education, *Social Studies K-12 Curriculum Guide*. Winnipeg, 1981.

N. McDonald & A. Chaiton (eds.), *Egerton Ryerson and his Times*. Toronto: Macmillan, 1978.

D. McKnight, *Moving Left: The Future of Socialism in Australia*. Sydney: Pluto, 1986.

P. McLaren, *Cries from the Corridor*. Toronto: Methuen, 1980.

P. McLaren, *Schooling as a Ritual Performance*. London: Routledge & Kegan Paul, 1986.

G. Milburn (ed.), *Teaching History in Canada*. Toronto: McGraw-Hill-Ryerson, 1972.

R. Miliband, *The State in Capitalist Society*. London: Weidenfeld & Nicolson, 1969.

W. Mishler, *Political Participation in Canada*. Toronto: McGraw-Hill-Ryerson, 1979.

F. Musgrove, *School and the Social Order*. Chichester: Wiley, 1979.

F. Newman, *Education for Citizen Action*. Berkeley: McCutchan, 1975.

J. Oakes, *Keeping Track: How Schools Structure Inequality*. New Haven: Yale University Press, 1985.

K.W. Osborne, *"Hard-working, Temperate and Peaceable": The Portrayal of Workers in Candian History Textbooks*. Winnipeg: University of Manitoba, 1980.

B. Palmer, *Working Class Experience: The Rise and Reconstitution of Canadian Labour 1800-1980*. Toronto: Butterworth, 1983.

C. Pateman, *Participation and Democratic Theory*. Cambridge: Cambridge University Press, 1970.

M. Ross, *The Impossible Sum of Our Traditions*. Toronto: McClelland & Stewart, 1986.

Saskatchewan Department of Education, *Report of the Social Sciences Reference Committee*. Regina, 1983.

D. Sawyer, *Tomorrow is School*. Vancouver: Douglas & MacIntyre, 1979.

J. Seabrook, *Working-Class Childhood: An Oral History*. London: Gallancz, 1982.

R. Sennett & J. Cobb, *The Hidden Injuries of Class*. New York: Knopf, 1972.

R. Sharp, *Knowledge, Ideology and the Politics of Schooling: Towards a Marxist Analysis of Education*. London: Routledge & Kegan Paul, 1980.

B. Simon, "Contemporary Problems in Educational Theory," *Marxism Today*, June 1976, pp. 169-177.

D. Smith, "Nationalism," in *The Canadian Encyclopedia*, Vol. II, pp. 1199-1200. Edmonton: Hurtig, 1985.

G. Snyders, *Ecole, classe et lutte des classes*. Paris: Presses universitaires de France, 1976.

T.H.B. Symons, *To Know Ourselves*. Toronto: A.U.C.C., 1975.

D.F. Thompson, *John Stuart Mill and Representative Government*. Princeton: Princeton University Press, 1976.

G.S. Tomkins, *A Common Countenance: Stability and Change in the Canadian Curriculum.* Toronto: Prentice-Hall, 1986.

B.S. Turner, *Citizenship and Capitalism.* London: Allen & Unwin, 1986.

G. Whitty, *Sociology and School Knowledge: Curriculum Theory, Research and Politics.* London: Methuen, 1985.

G. Whitty & M. Young, *Explorations in the Politics of School Knowledge.* Driffield: Nafferton Books, 1976.

R. Williams, *Culture and Society 1780-1950.* London: Chatto & Windus, 1968.

P. Willis, *Learning to Labour: How Working Class Kids Get Working Class Jobs.* Farnborough: Saxon House, 1976.

Winnipeg School District, *Annual Report,* 1913.

M. Young (ed.), *Knowledge and Control.* London: Collier-Macmillan, 1971.

M. Young & G. Whitty, *Society, State and Schooling.* Guildford: Falmer, 1977.

M. Yudkin (ed.), *General Education.* Harmondsworth: Penguin, 1971.

Join The Debate
On What Should Happen
In Canada's Schools

**The issues raised in books like this one
will be carried on the pages of
Our Schools/Our Selves
A Magazine for Canadian Education Activists.**

**The best way to keep in touch is to fill out one of the
subscription forms opposite and mail it in.**

But we hope you'll do more than read us. We hope you'll get involved in these issues, if you aren't already. And that you'll let us know what you think of our articles and books.

For a year's subscription you'll get 4 magazines and 4 books.

The next issue of the magazine (January 1989) will include:
Politics in the Elementary Classroom—An Anti-War-Toy Curriculum in Quebec—"Whole Language" in Nova Scotia—The BCTF, Solidarity and Vander Zalm—The Dangers of School-Based Budgeting—Teacher Training in Alberta—Teaching "General Level" Students—The Anti-Streaming Battle Heats Up in Ontario—Elementary Schooling in Vancouver 1920-1960—And a Prize Crossword for Education Junkies.

In the next couple of years you'll receive books on **The Crisis in Childcare—Curriculum Activists in Quebec—A Feminist Agenda for Canadian Schools—Streaming Working-Class Students in Ontario Schools—Heritage Languages in Canada—Native Education—Physical Education—The Culture of Childhood.** The subscription price for each of these books will be as much as 50% off the bookstore price.

Subscribe Today and Give
A Subscription Form To A Friend

Subscribe Today

It's time for a magazine that brings together education activists in our schools, our communities, and our unions... We need your support.

I want to subscribe to OUR SCHOOLS / OUR SELVES

☐ Regular   8 issues $32.00
☐ Student/Pensioner/Unemployed   8 issues $28.00
☐ Organization   8 issues $40.00

Sustaining (8 issues) ☐ $100 ☐ $200 ☐ $500 ☐ $_____

Please start with issue number [ ]

Name_____

Address _____

City _____Prov._____ Code_____

Cheque Enclosed ☐   Bill me later ☐
Visa/Mastercard ☐ Number_____

Expiry Date _____ Signature_____

Pass to a friend

It's time for a magazine that brings together education activists in our schools, our communities, and our unions... We need your support.

I want to subscribe to OUR SCHOOLS / OUR SELVES

☐ Regular   8 issues $32.00
☐ Student/Pensioner/Unemployed   8 issues $28.00
☐ Organization   8 issues $40.00

Sustaining (8 issues) ☐ $100 ☐ $200 ☐ $500 ☐ $_____

Please start with issue number [ ]

Name_____

Address _____

City _____Prov._____ Code_____

Cheque Enclosed ☐   Bill me later ☐
Visa/Mastercard ☐ Number_____

Expiry Date _____ Signature_____

**Business
Reply Mail**

No postage stamp
necessary if mailed
in Canada.

Postage will be paid by

OUR SCHOOLS/OUR SELVES
1698 Gerrard Street East,
Toronto, Ontario, CANADA
M4L 9Z9

**Business
Reply Mail**

No postage stamp
necessary if mailed
in Canada.

Postage will be paid by

OUR SCHOOLS/OUR SELVES
1698 Gerrard Street East,
Toronto, Ontario, CANADA
M4L 9Z9